David Gentleman's
PARIS

The Place de la Concorde

with my love and "happy birthday" wishes — and just a hint of many relaxed and relaxing returns ×××× lesley of the day. 27. 5. 91

DAR××××
&
i/d

The Pont Neuf and the Ile de la Cité

David Gentleman's
PARIS

A John Curtis Book
Hodder & Stoughton
LONDON SYDNEY AUCKLAND TORONTO

The Quai de Montebello

British Library Cataloguing in Publication Data

Gentleman, David, *1930*–
    David Gentleman's Paris.
    1. France, Paris, Description and Travel
    I Title
    914.43604838

    ISBN 0-340-51869-3

Published by Hodder and Stoughton,
a division of Hodder and Stoughton Ltd,
Mill Road, Dunton Green, Sevenoaks, Kent TN13 2YE
Editorial Office: 47 Bedford Square, London WC1B 3DP

Photoset by Rowland Phototypesetting Ltd, Suffolk
Colour separations by Dot Gradations, Essex

Printed in Italy by L.E.G.O., Vicenza

Contents

The Tuileries Gardens

Introduction

I had my first glimpse of Paris on a September day trip when I was a schoolboy of seventeen. I can remember only the big shed of the Gare St Lazare, and the Madeleine; the long hot arcades of the Rue de Rivoli, and eating a ham sandwich of crusty French bread on a bridge over the Seine. But later on, as a student, I stayed in the city several times and got to know it quite well; wandering the streets and quays and making pen-and-ink drawings in a spiral-bound sketchbook; sleeping mostly in cheap hotel rooms high up off the Boulevard St Germain, with washbasin and tin bidet always curtained off in one corner; and going in and out under the suspicious eyes of fat old *concierges.* Once I slept on a riverside bench under the trees; but though it felt romantic, it proved inconvenient and impractical to have no proper base. I lived happily enough off bread and tomatoes, cheese and grapes; I had no money for proper meals and looked longingly at the restaurant tables covered with clean paper table-cloths and set with sparkling glasses, all of which were of course quite out of my reach. But I'd read in an English paper that, if short of cash, one could still get a surprisingly good meal in France by marching into a restaurant, offering the waiter whatever one had to spare, and challenging him to do the best he could with it. In Paris this approach was not well received, and I only tried it once. But despite such minor setbacks I liked the city: the Métro signs and the sculptures in the Tuileries Gardens, the pretty cast-iron lamp-standards and the vivid all-night activity of Les Halles,

the now vanished central markets – their bloodstained and brutal-looking meat-porters notwithstanding. The city was fascinating. Not that I had much to compare it with apart from London, which in those days I hardly knew, it was the only capital city I'd ever seen. Probably what I most liked about it was the feeling of being abroad and Bohemian. But whatever the reason, Paris seemed to me quite magical.

When I go to Paris now, my delight and amazement on seeing the city's glories afresh – its green bronze columns topped by gilded figures, its palaces and leafy boulevards, its fine avenues and splendid public spaces – are as vivid as ever: such resources, so many good ideas, so many talented architects and sculptors to give them all shape. Many of these things I love unreservedly, even if now my reactions are occasionally tinged with a feeling of being overwhelmed; and also with the realisation that, tunnel or no tunnel, my native Albion, still in my youth so splendidly perfidious, has now grown by comparison marginal and provincial while France has stayed in the European mainstream. Yet looking and marvelling at the splendours of Paris – the Pont Alexandre III, the Eiffel Tower, the Grande Arche at La Défense – one realises that one is being worked on, got at: subjected to an almost overbearing concentration of spectacles, of sights intended specially to impress. All the most magnificent, the most impressive Parisian monuments – the Louvre, the Invalides, the Rue de Rivoli, the Pompidou Centre, the Pei Pyramid – have this element of glorification, whether of monarchs, emperors, heads of state, regimes or merely ministers. It's bound to make a Londoner feel overawed and shopkeeperish. Yet one can't help also feeling oppressed at the inhuman economic and administrative power that must have underpinned all this grandeur and orderliness and made it all possible. For what do all these fine monuments, all this magnificence celebrate if not hollow, discarded or extinct myths: absolute monarchy, militarism, religion, the benevolent altruism of business? What's more, the absolute power enshrined in the great Parisian monuments of the past, in the Invalides and the Louvre and the Salpêtrière, and implied in the new commercial palaces of today, has become an anachronism, a fiction; only an echo of what it used to be. The economic realities that matter now are more accurately expressed by the brand names – Toshiba, Mercedes, Bayer – which at night light up the Paris skyline: and there is nothing very French, let alone Parisian, about them.

So to be overwhelmed by Parisian monumental grandeur for its own sake is, in part at least, to fall for presentation – for a splendid bit of PR. But I feel no such reservations about the beautiful tall rows of houses, their façades tinted grey and cream and patterned with finely detailed shutters and balconies, their continuity broken here and there by arched entrances into hidden courtyards, or interrupted by the curving lines of a baroque church front. There is nothing overbearing or inhuman about the cafés and shops and markets, the buses and the Métro, the vivid life of the various districts, and the elegant or industrious and struggling existence of the people. These are the sharp true reminders of the real Parisian civilisation, of its human face.

In comparison with London or New York, Paris is not really very big, and it has not spread as far as they have: it still has real country round it. After Heathrow and the brief flight over suburban south-eastern England, the France you look down on during the descent into Charles de Gaulle still looks like a picture in the Duc de Berry's Book of Hours: a peasant landscape, open and rural, with strip fields, a château, well-spaced villages and farmsteads joined up by white roads across the coloured countryside. On the final approach you see a new motorway and some red and white pylons, but as you touch down even the airfield itself looks rural – falcons

Soup kitchen, Tour St Jacques

The terrace of the Palais de Chaillot

hovering by the runway, rows of perimeter poplars that Pissarro or Monet might have painted. Once inside the terminal though, everything changes to the present, or rather to period 'modern': you are processed through plastic tubes like a laboratory rat, bussed to a fine concrete railway station built like a vaulted cloister, and whisked off by the RER, the fast new suburban arm of the Métro, to central Paris in less time than the Heathrow tube takes to get into South Ealing. On the way the RER shoots you through dense and dreary suburbia and past tall blocks topped with sky signs for Nissan and Volvo – names that you notice in the same instant that you catch sight of the domes of the Sacré-Cœur and the distant Eiffel Tower.

The size of Paris makes it possible to see it whole – to take it all in as it were in one eyeful. From the modest heights of Montmartre or Belleville one can see right across the city as if from the rim of a dish, getting in the process an unforgettable impression of a vast leaden sea of roofs – largely unrelieved by greenery – and of the spires, towers, domes and tower blocks that rise out of it like ships or rocks. If one prefers one can choose a higher and more central bird's-eye view from the Eiffel Tower or the Tour Montparnasse. From the top of the Arc de Triomphe one can see along Haussmann's grandiose avenues as if looking along the spokes of a wheel from its hub. Then there are more intimate views of the central city roofscape from the top of the Pompidou Centre, reached by its spectacular free escalator, or much more laboriously from the walk-up towers of Notre-Dame. Another two excellent viewing points, this time complete with refreshment, may be enjoyed from the roof-top cafés of two big department stores, Au Printemps and Samaritaine. This last has the best Parisian view of all, over to the Ile de la Cité and the Left bank and down onto the Pont Neuf and all the varied and ceaseless river traffic of the Seine.

Paris is sufficiently compact for you to be able to walk to many of the places you want to see without wearing yourself out. Yet within this quite modest area, Parisian layout and design are monumental indeed. As a pedestrian one passes through great arches that dwarf even the scurrying traffic; one walks past classical façades of cold perfection, along wide avenues, straight and tree-lined; and one enjoys, on the way, startling glimpses down streets and boulevards, with vistas and perspectives which end in distant domes or towers or spires. At first, these happy effects seem like accidents. But they are not: all this had to be skilfully and purposefully, even quite ruthlessly, contrived. Even the most romantic and apparently haphazard features, like the mountain of rocks in the Buttes Chaumont Park, turn out to be the ingenious works not of nature but of man – and built, what's more, out of unlikely material: old rubbish tips and heaps of bones.

The Parisians have been very good at creating such visual delights. They have managed it partly by cunningly enhancing what was there already – the river especially – but partly by the most brilliant and inventive creation. One of their most fertile techniques has been to use or if necessary invent forms that are not merely striking in themselves but have a double role: for example, things that can be seen *through* – the Arc de Triomphe or the Carrousel or the Porte Saint-Denis or the transparent Pei Pyramid – or seen *around* – the Vendôme column, the Concorde obelisk – or seen *between* – the long lines of clipped trees in the Palais Royal, the Jardin des Plantes and the Luxembourg Gardens – or seen *underneath* – the pretty bridges, the great arch of the Eiffel Tower or the new Défense arch. I have seen no other city where such devices have been so widely and so skilfully deployed. It is this combination of imagination and ruthlessness that gives Paris its unique character.

Fame on a Winged Horse

The Institut de France

Wandering about the city makes one curious about its past. Signs of it keep surfacing everywhere, and as a Londoner one is bound to wonder how all this grandeur can have come about, since the two cities started off with so much in common. Both were originally river crossings which later grew into ports; both began as tribal settlements; both were occupied by the Romans; both were enclosed within a fortified wall of which sections (Roman in London, medieval in Paris) can still be seen. Both cities developed in separate, distinct parts with different functions. In London, the City was the commercial centre and Westminster the seat of Crown and Church; in Paris, commerce established itself on the right bank of the Seine and learning, under the authority of the Church, on the left. And naturally both cities grew outwards around their central cores, like swelling fruit, both cities proving equally difficult to confine. But the growth was contained in different ways, so that the outward spread of Paris can be traced and understood more logically and precisely than London's more haphazard sprawl.

The pressure outwards can be guessed at from the fact that the successive perimeter walls for containing Paris have been variously described as belts, corsets, walnut shells and garrottes, and the city's concentric layers within them as a set of Russian dolls. The walls were mainly military and were defensive in purpose. Defences had begun simply enough with the fortification of the banks of the Parisii's early settlement on the Ile de la Cité. The Philippe Auguste wall of about 1200 enclosed areas first on the right bank and then on the left. About 1380 the Charles V ramparts were built round the growing city's northern and eastern perimeters, taking in the now vanished fortress of the Bastille. This wall, which stood roughly on the line of the present-day Grands Boulevards from the Bastille to the Portes St Martin and St Denis, was extended westwards in the sixteenth century to include the palace of the Louvre. In 1784–91 a new wall, further out still, was built for fiscal reasons by the tax-collecting Farmers-General; unpopular and provocative, it quickly vanished in the Revolution but several of its fifty-seven handsome tollhouses remain, notably the fine Rotonde de la Villette and another at the entrance to the Parc

Monceau. Although the next perimeter, the Thiers fortifications of 1841–5, was built in response to a military threat, it quickly proved itself completely useless as a defence against heavy cannon. The difference between threatened, continental Paris and secure, offshore London becomes clear if one tries to imagine Victorian London enclosed within an unbroken ring of ramparts, bastions and no-man's-land at roughly the radius of Hampstead or Clapham. Nevertheless, useless or not, the Thiers fortifications and the empty *cordon sanitaire* beyond them were effective at least in defining the city limits of the time; and in a ghostly way they still do so, in the shape of the Boulevard Périphérique, itself an unpleasant sort of no-man's-land, which is now their most prominent visible legacy.

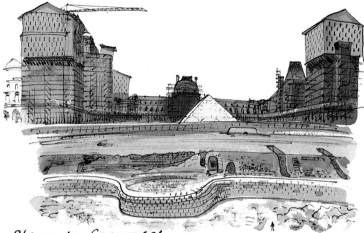

Place du Carrousel

But even having grasped the essential fact of the inexorable spread of Paris, despite which the city remained more or less circular in shape, it is still not always easy to date or place even roughly in period the buildings contained within these onion-skin layers. The Louvre for example has been growing and changing continuously from the time of Philippe Auguste until the present-day addition of the Pei Pyramid. Some surviving buildings can however be associated with more precise periods or dates, so that they can vividly evoke a century or a historical period. For example, from the twelfth century remain one or two towers and fragments of Philippe Auguste's wall, and the recently excavated foundations of the Louvre fortress. Of the Seine bridges, the Pont Neuf of 1578–1604 is the oldest. More ambitious planning – the Place des Vosges, the Luxembourg Gardens and Palace and the Tuileries, and the development of the Ile St Louis and of the Marais – all date from the seventeenth century. But even such masterpieces of planning as the Place Vendôme took longer to realise than one might think. The buildings date from the early eighteenth century, but its column from the time of Napoleon. Even the Arc de Triomphe, commissioned by the Emperor and thus heavily Napoleonic in spirit, was not finished until 1830.

On the other hand, much that now seems most

characteristically Parisian dates from a specific and quite brief period in the mid-nineteenth century. What's more, it came about in very unpromising circumstances. After the 1830 and 1848 revolutions, Baron Haussmann set about transforming the city by driving new boulevards through the old dissident working-class areas in order to make them easier to control during riots. In this pitiless process he destroyed much that was ancient and shabby but also interesting and beautiful; including, incidentally, many small private gardens. He replaced narrow and winding streets with the wide straight boulevards and the mechanically repetitive façades that the Impressionists later made familiar. The whole destructive process was redeemed by the double lines of trees squeezed out along the complete length of the boulevards like toothpaste from a tube – providing foliage which now lightens the monotony with shade and freshness. For luckily Haussmann's ruthlessness was tempered with imagination: to him we owe not just the bombastic Champs-Elysées but the Parcs Monceau and Montsouris (to compensate perhaps for all the lost gardens), the tidying-up of the Bois de Boulogne, and the beautiful Parc des Buttes Chaumont. What Haussmann really represents is the nineteenth-century drive for order: he deserves to be thought of as a more complex, less brutal figure than in the past. And then after him, the later nineteenth century brought the big railway stations and the fine commercial buildings near the Bourse, and mechanical and commercial marvels like the Eiffel Tower and the Métro. Much of what is most Parisian, much of what I most like about the city is nineteenth century.

The twentieth, though, has been generally destructive to Paris, bringing the scourges of suburbia, cars and mass tourism without any such lucky spin-offs as the emergence of figures like Haussmann to right the balance. In architecture, curiously enough, the modern movement made less of an impression on the city than it did in painting and sculpture. In recent years there has been such pressure on space that new building in the centre has been largely restricted to either filling in small gaps or artificially creating new spaces for redevelopment by razing everything to the ground – beyond the Gare d'Austerlitz, for instance – or simply by digging deep beneath the surface, as at the Louvre and Les Halles. The last years of the century are being marked both by a new concern for the past and by a remarkably bold attempt to think and plan clearly for the future: to this end, the Pavillon de l'Arsenal offers a fascinating permanent exhibition explaining the city's past and its future prospects.

It's hard, if one likes a city, to put one's finger precisely on any single reason why: it is the whole which makes the impression, not the parts. But some Parisian pleasures are easily identified. I like the Métro – not just Guimard's cast-iron station entrances but the whole thing. It was well designed to begin with, and its stations have not been too badly knocked about by recent face-lifts. I like it where it surfaces into the fresh air and trundles along on grey girders at first-floor level, and its daring river crossings, higher still on a top deck above an ordinary road bridge; and even its cheeky mid-air intrusion over the trees of the Parc Montsouris.

I love the open spaces, the Luxembourg Gardens especially, and the many smaller *places* (no adequate English translation exists), and their undefiled grass – even if the price one pays for this is having to keep off it, or at any rate not lying down on it, and getting whistled at by fierce park policemen if one disobeys. I like watching the sociable open-air pastimes of the parks – chess, cards, ping-pong on solid concrete tables, and the merry-go-rounds and the home-made toy sailing boats hired out by the hour by nut-brown attendants in yachting caps.

I like the walks – by the Canal St Martin, by the Invalides and the Ecole Militaire, in the Jardin des Plantes, along the quays. I like the Parisian skyline, marked by its domes and spires, with only here and there a cluster of skyscrapers; and the sea of roofs, of blue-grey slate and sun-whitened zinc. I like the famous sights, the great historic set-pieces: the fine mansions like the Hôtel Sully, and the use made of their courtyards by musicians and actors, and the mysterious tantalising glimpses into such places through creeper-hung arches or half-open doorways; and all the venerable bric-à-brac of grandeur – arches, domes, terraces, theatrical bits of sculpture. But I also love the minor architectural survivors: the old corner bakers' shops and the dairies that still display gilded signs for eggs, butter and cheese; and the big thirties' cinemas, and the tiny shoebox-sized ones too. I like the complacent opulence of the nineteenth-century banks and churches, and the greedy splendour of the big commercial buildings in the Rue Réaumur; and the older, innocently uncommercial grandeur of the fine seventeenth-century buildings and courtyards in the Marais and the Faubourg St Germain. I marvel at the skilful but discreet upkeep of all such historic buildings; but also, and not unrelated to this, at the courage, the optimistic pride and eagerness with which good – and, admittedly, bad – new buildings are welcomed, from architects who are by no means all French. And as a Londoner, I especially admire not just the style and confidence of such individual masterpieces as the Institute of the Arab World, but the city's willingness to revitalise whole run-down areas such as La Villette, and the skill and resourcefulness with which the job is being done.

I also enjoy Paris for its surprises: like that curious island, the long straight-as-a-die Allée des Cygnes, and the Buttes Chaumont park with its happy Japanese newly-weds being photographed by the lake; and the Pagoda café near Montparnasse; and the mysterious names and individuality of all the various quarters or districts: the Marais and Montparnasse and St Denis and Passy and La République and La Défense.

But I also love ordinary daily life in Paris: the profusion of good cafés with tables on the pavement, and the restaurants, and the standard of brasserie food (good salads, good camembert or gruyère with butter in a crisp split-open baguette), and the good service, and the theatricality of the beautiful black-and-white uniform of the waiters. I like the streets: the clear traffic-lighting of the crossings and the concern for pedestrians; and the fascinating Parisian pavement details: the Wallace fountains, the Morris columns, the lovely wooden public benches, the iron notice-boards and the metal gates that clang solidly shut behind you as you enter a park; and I like the lacy cast-iron collars round the tree trunks, and the public loos with their matter-of-fact guardian ladies; and their opposites, the old spikily patterned corner railings that mean 'don't you dare to pee here'.

There are some Parisian sounds I like to hear: the creaking and straining sound of a great wooden door being heaved open early in the morning, the frantic whistles of the traffic policemen, the Métro hooter just before the doors shut, swifts shrieking high in the summer air, kestrels crying round the spire of Notre-Dame, the sound of crickets in the crevices in the warm quayside walls and the two-tone electronic call-sign *boing-doing* of the *bateaux-mouches* in the long summer evenings.

I like the museums: the Orsay, the Cluny, the Carnavalet, and the general respect accorded to the idea of Art. I like especially the good use made of gardens and *places*, the Place des Vosges for instance, by high-spirited parties of schoolchildren, and the bits of green grass, not just trodden-on mud, in the parks, and the *boules* games wherever there's a stretch of sand. And I love the things that give the city style: the big dignified un-tarted-up railway stations, and the nice green buses, especially the ones which are once again open to the elements at the back.

The Brasserie Flo

The Pont Neuf

Most of all I love the river, its bridges of stone, bronze, iron and steel, and its quays, so beautifully angled and sloping, so subtly curving, so bare in winter, so luxuriant with weeds in spring; and the planes and willows and chestnuts that shade them. And I like the climate, and the seasons, and the ever-changing effects of light. And especially in the warmest parts of the year (a period which seems presently to be extending) I love the spectacle of Parisian life being lived in the open air, visible and uninhibited: people shopping, eating, drinking, begging, playing music, performing, being lazy, sleeping, everything going on in full view; the couples everywhere, sitting on the river banks or on the metal seats in the Luxembourg Gardens, or still enjoying each other's company over the breakfast croissants; and the enjoyment and the expectancy in the air everywhere. And there is something else too, more intangible but real enough even so: a pervasive sense of history, of 1789, and an inherited readiness to strive for a better way to live, an attitude evidently accepted in Paris as natural and sensible, not as a target for automatic cynicism and ridicule.

But of course there are things to be deplored too. Cars have changed the appearance of every street, turning them into teeming torrents of metal or clogged sewers choking with exhaust fumes as the cars grind to a smelly standstill. Traffic has turned much of the Right Bank of the Seine into a noisy motorway cutting everyone off from the river, and it had designs on the Left Bank which were only partly thwarted. And parked cars and motorcycles have filched every spare – or not spare – metre of pavement from people and trees.

Another destructive intrusion is the rapid Americanisation of many cafés and shops. It's not so much that there is anything wrong with junk food but simply that each new Burger King inevitably replaces something local and individual with something universal, making the street less interesting, less Parisian. Bit by bit, but relentlessly and fast, Whoppers, Burgers, Big Macs and their like are replacing the curious, unpredictable, *different* kind of city one had gone hoping to find with a place one already knows only too well.

The principal drawback is the development of tourism. No one who enjoys going abroad can afford to complain about how other visitors are spoiling things. But even as a tourist oneself one can't help being aware of how the industry that has shipped one in, with its sharp eye for exploiting and vulgarising the city's landmarks and experiences, is not merely transforming them into spectacle, business and cash, but destroying them into the bargain. Montmartre is the most outrageous instance of this dispiriting and destructive process: fun if you are in the right frame of mind, awful if you aren't.

There are naturally enough other minor things I don't particularly like: the self-importance seeping from the ridiculous tombs in the cemetery of Père Lachaise; the Centre Pompidou, which already looks not just self-assertive and architecturally immature but very shabby too; the whole pointless redevelopment of Les Halles; and the triumphalism of the Invalides, the Ecole Militaire and the Arc de Triomphe: who now gives a toss for Triumph? Then there are some conspicuous little errors of taste like the silly broken-off columns stuck about in the courtyard of the Palais Royal, and some unfortunate big ones like the hideously patterned skyscrapers of the Front de Seine. All these seem to me things more to be regretted than admired.

And Paris is expensive. Even if hotel rooms are still relatively cheap, living there as a visitor, even quite modestly, is not. Cafés and restaurants and all aspects of daily life are dear. But it can be worth it: at a café you are paying not just for the drink and the service but also for space and spectacle, for the enjoyment of a marvellous scene – and maybe, if you happen to be drawing, for a convenient workplace too.

Paris is a very good city for an artist to work in. It is a bit warmer than London, but seldom too hot to draw outside; the summer evenings are light and long. Parisian distances being short, one can walk to one's subject, taking in the look of the place on the way; and afterwards one can walk back in the detached yet receptive frame of mind that comes after a day's drawing, and see new subjects or new rearrangements of familiar ones or things one somehow missed before. This perpetual reappraisal, the gradual discovery of what is most *worth* drawing, is a slow but necessary process, one which can't be hurried; and here it is a pleasure too.

What's more, the French are tolerant of painters and their clobber; they are accepted as normal, not as oddities or freaks. Artists of all sorts are found dotted about here and there on the bridges and the quays. Of course, drawing in the open, you may well find that someone else has got there first, or that a photographer is using the same scene – and not necessarily one of the more obvious ones – as a background for a fashion shot. Indeed, drawing in Paris, as in Venice, one soon begins to feel uneasily aware that everything, *everything*, has been noticed, drawn, painted, photographed already – often. But this is only half-true. The look of the place is changing all the time; buildings disappear, lights and seasons vary, the people and the clothes look different on each new visit. In any case, what does it matter if something has been drawn already by someone else? One's own discoveries, experiences and reactions are what count.

The city is interesting to draw because of its contrasts: of old with new, of grandeur with curious and intimate detail, of cash and pomp with poverty and energy. It looks good because of the changes of light, weather, season; because of its clipped trees and grey walls; because of the fascination and surprises of the passing scene, and the spectacle of so much vitality on display. Drawing it, one comes to realise that Paris looks the way it does because of the seemingly casual but determined ways in which people have shaped it to their needs and tastes, making it into what they most want it to be: a place for working, or eating and drinking, or parking the car, or studying, or buying and selling, or showing off, or just flopping in the sun. Imposing or relaxed, showy or unconcerned, grandiose or intimate, traditional or avant-garde, things look well here.

Through a Londoner's eyes they also look clean and well cared for. Evidently the city must have more self-respect and more self-confidence than London, as well as a healthy scepticism about the efficacy of market forces. In looking after itself, Paris is proud, clean and thorough. It has for instance a vast fleet of green street-cleaning trucks to wash the place down several times a day, a fleet so specialised that it includes vehicles that, having emptied your dustbin, wash and scrub it out too. And its public services are well thought-out and efficient. The Métro and the buses, which the city helps to pay for, have not been broken up and sold off. Instead, they work well. The airport and the business district of La Défense are served by the fast new RER – compare London's toy tramway to Dockland and the lack of any land link at all to the City Airport. And now there are plans for an underground expressway deep below the centre of the city.

But beyond these practical virtues is something more intangible. The most exhilarating aspect of Paris is the self-confidence and enthusiasm, the feeling that every experience – the setting, the people, the occasion – will be relished and made the most of. The essential and unique Parisian achievement has been the purposeful creation of a *communal* place, rational and ordered and able somehow to harness *for the general benefit* the natural energies that exist wherever people live together. Such a place has attracted talented, lively, alert and demanding people who have made Paris good to look at and to live in: a civilised place existing alongside the famous monuments, but separate and independent from them.

All the same, there is in my experience a drawback. Paris is indeed a beautiful and life-enhancing city. But because its vigour and variety, its verve, shake one up, it is also an unsettling one. Visiting Paris makes one reassess one's own ingrained and comfortable habits, views and assumptions. If this prospect seems a little risky, think it over: it might perhaps be safer not to go.

The Pont au Double

Front de Seine from the Pont Mirabeau

The Seine

The Seine is not simply the city's finest natural feature, it is the most inescapable. Unlike the Hudson and the East River, which many New Yorkers know about but don't see much, and unlike the Thames, which many think of as London's southern boundary, the Seine is in the middle of everything. Parisian life flows as easily across it as along it. It is well used and carefully looked after, and it is a source of great beauty. Of interest and curiosity too, since it is also a port and a working waterway, used by clusters of coal, sand and rubbish barges and long petrol tankers as well as by many kinds of pleasure boats: rubber inflatables, yachts, Dutch barges and *bateaux-mouches*. Some of these last have now grown so vast that they look like aircraft carriers; in consequence, one of the city's prettiest bridges, the Pont des Arts, has had to be rebuilt with fewer but bigger arches to let them through. But this has been done so cleverly that no one would ever know.

The Seine is more than just the river itself. Its stone quays offer peace, relaxation and escape from the restless city pavements – though, it must be said, they have also provided the route for the disastrous expressway, the Voie Georges Pompidou, that has ruined the Right Bank. Elsewhere the quays have kept something of the same charm as canal towpaths, and even many of the same details: overgrown banks, ducks and ducklings in season, moored barges and iron rings for tying them up at; gently sloping ramps and steeper stone steps down the angled and overgrown quaysides into a river which is clear and clean enough for one to see waterweed and shoals of big fish moving in the current.

The quays have many uses. On summer mornings people do callisthenics under the bridges; when the weather is hot, sunbathers bask on the stones as if on the beach, or use the angled walls as deck-chairs; on summer evenings the quays become the haunt of drummers, tramps, winos, lovers and amateur saxophonists. One of the natural advantages of the Seine is that since it is not tidal, its water-level remains steady; it does not ebb away twice a day to reveal, far down below, a shamingly muddy and refuse-strewn bottom. And though the river is in some places just a big wide boring expanse of water like the Thames, in others – especially in the centre of the city where the islands split it in two – it becomes smaller, gentler and more intimate. Here the Seine is so narrow that, approaching it from the streets of the Left Bank, you can look across it without realising it's there at all, so near at hand are the buildings on the farther bank. And here too it is crossed by pretty stone bridges of quite modest size that would not look out of place in, say, Cambridge.

But the Seine has its industrial aspects too. The vanished Citroën factory used to stand on its bank, Renault on one of the islands: its old buildings still seem to float there in midstream under a plume of steam, like a Mississippi stern-wheeler. And the city's newest developments are taking place along the upstream river banks at the Quai de la Rapée, Bercy and at Seine Rive Gauche. The brand-new Finance Ministry even stands with its front feet in the Seine, as if to emphasise the interrelation of river and city. It's not a river you ignore.

The Ile Seguin

The Allée des Cygnes

The Allée des Cygnes is a shady tunnel of chestnuts running from end to end of a long narrow island. The place has a macabre history: it used to be a dump for the bodies of dead horses, the equivalent of today's breaker's yard. The island was built up in the 1830s and has the same remorseless straight-as-a-die rigidity as the Champs-Elysées or the Rue de Rivoli. On the May mid-morning when I drew it the place was fresh and beautiful beneath the chestnut candles, with a few strollers and dog-walkers; big fish were splashing about just where the stones of the island slope into the water.

The Allée des Cygnes

The Pont de Bir-Hakeim

Passy and the Pont Alexandre III

The Allée des Cygnes ends at the Pont de
Bir-Hakeim, which carries the Métro across
the river into the curious domed landscape
opposite. This is one of my favourite
Parisian views, because of its oddity, its
surreal mixing of the practical utilitarian
railway with the fairy-tale skyline beyond,
and its originality – all its elements seem
newly invented and surprising, not just
studious or reverent reworkings of the past.
The bridge carries some cast-iron allegorical
figures but you need a boat to see them.
All in all, it's beautiful, but not pretty;
whereas the Pont Alexandre III, two
kilometres upstream, however frivolous
in its decoration, is graceful *and* pretty:
its curving steel span clean and elegant,
its bronze figures like a piece of skilful
yet tongue-in-cheek window-display.

The Pont Alexandre III

21

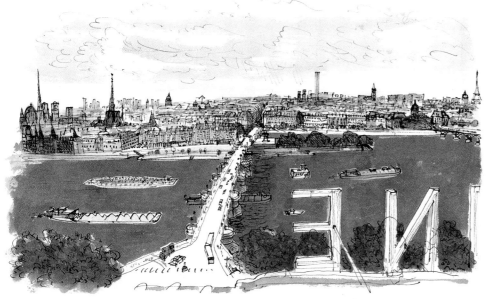

The Pont Neuf from the Quai de la Mégisserie

The Pont Neuf from the roof of La Samaritaine

The Pont Neuf and the Square du Vert Galant

The Pont Neuf is venerable and sturdy, its pointed piers slicing through the olive-brown river, its sides embellished with grotesque and too-lovingly restored antique heads, now robbed of any mystery or ambiguity. However you look at it, the bridge is curious; sometimes it is beautiful. I like its distant prospect from the corner where the Pont au Change meets the Quai de la Mégisserie; however far away, it nevertheless forms the foreground in one of those triple-element views in which the city abounds, backed as it is here by the dome of the Institut de France and the distant Eiffel Tower, making a last appearance as one heads upstream.

The Pont Neuf is in two halves, slightly misaligned where they meet on the Ile de la Cité. The northern half of the bridge leads straight to the Samaritaine department store, named after the figure on a hydraulic pump that used to supply the Louvre with water. From the store's roof-top café one can see through the gigantic letters of its sign, across the Seine to the Left Bank. This splendid view takes in some key Parisian landmarks: the skyline of Notre-Dame; the sharp spire of the Sainte-Chapelle rising from its prison, ignominiously boxed in by the Palais de Justice; the dome of the distant Panthéon; the two asymmetric towers of the church of St Sulpice; and beyond them the Montparnasse tower, the city's second skyscraper, and the Eiffel Tower, its first. On the far quay stand the Hôtel des Monnaies (the Mint) and the nobly domed Institut de France. Below is the Seine, busy with a curious mixture of craft – sand barges, lighters, petroleum tankers, and puny-looking little tugs that can still push four laden barges in front of them. There are also various pleasure boats, mostly *bateaux-mouches*, many of which now look too big to squeeze under the bridges. One of the largest has a retractable wheelhouse that shrinks down into the hull as it approaches each bridge, provided the pilot remembers in time.

The bridge crosses the Ile de la Cité near its pointed downstream tip, which juts into the Seine, dividing its waters like the prow – or in this instance the stern – of a ship. The decks of this 'ship' are reached by stairs down from the Place du Pont Neuf. The upper deck, the beautiful Square du Vert Galant or Elderly Adventurer, an allusion to the amorous Henri IV, is a narrow triangular lawn surrounded by big trees. The lower deck is the surrounding quay, its sides shelving away into the water.

The tip of the Square du Vert Galant

The Pont Neuf

The Quai des Grands Augustins from the Quai des Orfevres

The Quai des Orfèvres and the Quai des Grands Augustins

Where the wide Seine is divided by the two islands, it changes character. Each channel is narrower, the southern one more markedly so and more tranquil, seeming almost a backwater. Beside it and just upstream from the Pont Neuf is the Quai des Orfèvres. Down by the water's edge it is sheltered from traffic noise and offers a hard but serviceable stone beach to bask on when it is really hot. Half-hidden on the left of the drawing are the unappealing walls and towers of the Palais de Justice and the forbidding police headquarters. On the opposite bank stand the tall houses of the Quai des Grands Augustins, their clifflike fronts rounded off at the top by that characteristic Parisian feature, the zinc-covered mansard roof. These give the buildings a curiously pumped-up look, which appears in its most startling form round the Place St Michel, in the middle distance of the drawing. This is a good place to walk at any time; in summer especially so, when the sloping quaystones and the green water below are both luxuriant with their different growing plants – or were until the quay was resurfaced in 1990. In the morning the place tends to be deserted, with only a few people walking or reading. On hot afternoons sunbathers, complete with bathing towels and beachbags, take over the quays, just as in London they take over the park grass, something which here is forbidden them. Set into the quayside walls are big iron rings so that barges can tie up; in the evening these walls retain the day's warmth and crickets chirp from the crevices between the stones.

Printseller on the Quai de Montebello

The Quai des Grands Augustins and the Quai de Montebello

The most animated stretch of the Seine quays is between the Pont St Michel and the Pont au Double. The pavements hereabouts are lined with the heavy lock-up cases of the *bouquinistes* or print-sellers on the quayside walls, often so close-set that you only catch glimpses of the river where there is a gap between the stalls or a flight of steps down to the lower quay. It is this two-tiered life that gives charm to these central quays: the traffic and the commerce up at street level, the leisurely and almost trance-like pleasure in one's surroundings down below at water level. It can be seen in the drawing opposite on the Quai des Grands Augustins, looking towards the Pont Neuf. Here the lower (quayside) level is open to the sky. The drawing was made on a September morning when the summer crowds had thinned. In the new development upstream from the Pont St Michel, on pages 28–29, the Quai

St Michel undercuts the pavement and is in consequence already dark and smelly.

The *bouquinistes*' boxes are compact and solidly built green wooden cases with a waterproof zinc roof; three or four together constitute one owner's pitch. Early in the morning, and indeed throughout the day at quieter times of year, they are padlocked shut. When the owner arrives, he or she unlocks the boxes, unfolds the lids and props them open on metal uprights, and pins or clips the pretty coloured prints onto them. The heavier books remain stacked within the box; bigger prints are sometimes laid in an X-shaped portfolio that stands on the pavement. The whole process of setting out the display from such modest and unpromising beginnings is like the spreading of a peacock's tail. When it is complete, the owner retreats to a deck-chair on the farther side of the pavement, from where – with the watchful air not so much of the

peacock as of the spider – he or she can survey the range of cases and the reactions of the passers-by. The owner of the boxes above, on the Quai de Montebello opposite the Square Viviani, gets up from her seat every now and then, hammer in hand, to break up some dried crusts of bread for the pigeons on the wall.

The Pont St Michel

BATEAUX-MOUCHES

The Pont Alexandre III

Six Parisian bridges

Paris is not short of bridges. Between the Pont de Grenelle and the Pont de Bercy there are twenty-eight of them, for pedestrians or traffic or railways, sometimes for all three. Some, like the Pont Alexandre III, are beautiful and graceful in themselves; others, like the Pont Royal, are interesting only as part of a familiar Parisian landscape – in this instance, the flamboyant late-nineteenth-century rooflines of the later Louvre and the Gare (now Musée) d'Orsay opposite.

The Pont Neuf, finished in 1604, is the oldest, though it has been restored so often that it doesn't look it. Where it crosses the Ile de la Cité, two fine houses mark the entrance to the triangular Place Dauphine.

The next bridge upstream on the Right Bank side is the Pont au Change, so called because it used to be occupied by moneylenders and jewellers. Beyond it rise the oppressive walls and towers of the Conciergerie. These look picturesque enough, but they have a grim resonance: the furthest pointed tower is called the Bonbec or Babbler's Tower from its old function of torture chamber. The bridge connects the island with the Quai de la Mégisserie, which meant Tannery Quay; its caged prisoners are still there, tier upon

The Pont Neuf

The Pont de Sully

The Pont Royal

tier of rabbits and pigeons and poultry.

Further upstream again on the north Right Bank is the Pont Louis-Philippe, rebuilt in 1862. It is a handsome but coldly correct structure, its chief visual function being to provide a foil to the church of St Gervais-St Protais which rises to the north of it. At any time of year this seems to me a beautiful scene, with the old upright church, the later houses, and the pompous

but not insufferable stone bridge.

The upstream tip of the Ile St Louis is joined to both Left and Right Banks by the cast-iron Pont de Sully. Only the piers here are of stone, and they are unadorned: to its designers, the metal arches must have seemed interesting enough shapes in their own right. Beneath it, barges and pleasure craft tie up at the Port de la Tournelle quayside. Beyond it rise two much more

recent metal structures, the tall square tower of the Universités Paris VI–Paris VII by the Place Jussieu and the beautiful Institut du Monde Arabe, a distinguished and elegant building which makes the Pompidou Centre look a bit hamfisted. You can visit the Institut after midday; its roof terrace has one of the best views on the river.

The Pont au Change

The Pont Louis-Philippe

31

The Quai d'Orléans

The Ile St Louis

The Ile de la Cité and the Ile St Louis are separated by a channel under the Pont St Louis which the *bateaux-mouches* never use, but which is often busy with other craft: police launches, long, low tankers and strings of sand barges. The view here is taken looking across this channel, towards the Quai d'Orléans. The low waterside quay seen emerging from the Seine is pretty but short-lived – it comes to an end round the corner, before reaching the Pont de la Tournelle on the right of the drawing. It is a delightful and sunny place; its few wooden benches are broken and smelly, but one can sit on the angle of the quay, or on the steps leading down into the water. In the distance are the recently built offices on the Quai de la Rapée, behind the Gare de Lyon.

The barge in the foreground is pushing through the water with a characteristic wave that one quickly comes to recognise.

The Seine from the Pont de la Tournelle

35

The Île St Louis - the Quai de Bourbon

The Pont de Bercy

The Pont Marie and Bercy

Upstream from the Pont Marie is the Quai d'Anjou, the most placid and most rural stretch of riverside in central Paris – provided one ignores the Right Bank Expressway just opposite. This shortish stretch of quay is screened from the fine seventeenth-century houses above it by stone walls and foliage. It leads nowhere in particular, so it's quiet: people walk their dogs here, lovers stroll and tramps can sleep undisturbed. With its five rounded arches, each a slightly different shape, the graceful bridge might be in a quiet provincial town.

But further upstream, beyond the Pont d'Austerlitz on the Quai de la Rapée, the Seine turns firmly back into a no-nonsense working port again. Angular construction machinery and conveyors stand like giant insects in front of half-demolished nineteenth-century warehouses, relics whose romantic silhouettes are giving way to the gleaming metal office blocks in front of the Gare de Lyon. Beyond is the beautiful Pont de Bercy, which in 1990 was being widened. It is a magnificent hybrid, a mixture of grandeur and practicality, with echoes both of its venerable all-stone relative

the Pont du Gard, and of the all-metal Pont de Bir-Hakeim far downstream. Like the latter it is a double-decker to carry the Métro; both make this utilitarian role the pretext for a magnificent structure.

Just visible over the train is the brand-new Finance Ministry, a tall and enormously long block crouched like a sphinx with its front paws in the water. Before I saw it I'd heard a ministry official, uprooted from his desirable old office in the Louvre, complaining about this deplorable banishment to the sticks. But the move is

a psychologically important step in the renewal of the run-down eastern half of the city. Another such step is the siting just over the bridge of a big new sports stadium, the Palais Omnisports de Paris-Bercy; and soon a waterside park will be created, following the line of the river upstream. But for the present, the Seine here still retains its semi-industrial aspect. Sand barges so heavily laden that they are awash tie up at the quay and are later towed away again empty, bobbing and banging about high up on the water like empty tin cans.

imentation

produits
naturels

AU VIEUX PARIS

DIDIER

grotte galerie

claude d

The Rue de l'Échaudé

The Left Bank

Seen from the river, the southern or Left Bank presents an orderly frontage: an almost continuous strip of tall houses rising over a ground floor of shops and restaurants, its continuity broken here and there by small squares and *places* and by two large and dignified institutions, the Mint and the Institut de France. But immediately behind this stately façade there is surprising disorder and one can see here remnants of medieval muddle of a kind to be found nowhere else in the city: narrow twisting streets, ancient churches, small bars and restaurants selling Greek, Indonesian, Chinese and Tunisian food, and crowds of hungry visitors in retreat from the gastronomic wasteland around Notre-Dame. This is also an area of small street markets, some of them daily, others once a week. I like these small warren-like streets; this is where I used to stay as a student and an area to which I have often returned since. But it has become fashionable, and its agreeable muddle has been cashed in on by the decorators and the antique shops of a now smart and expensive district.

The Latin Quarter was so named not because of any southern or Romanesque associations but simply because, being the students' district, it was where Latin was spoken. But although the University was founded in 1253, and its church has a splendid baroque dome, and though the Place de la Sorbonne in front of it is handsome and lively, the Sorbonne's premises now are mainly nineteenth century and unromantic in the extreme. The Left Bank has a number of other notable domes: the most handsome monument on the Left Bank is the Institut de France with its fine Jesuit-style dome by Le Vau. The best way to approach it is by crossing the beautiful pedestrian Pont des Arts, thickly populated with artists, its wooden deck in summer a sort of bazaar for prints, cheap jewellery, knick-knacks, nuts, ice-cream, warm soft drinks and lightning friendships.

The Left Bank has two fine open spaces, the Jardin des Plantes and the Jardin du Luxembourg, and it is crossed by two notable thoroughfares. The Boulevard St Michel or Boul' Mich, now brash and rather vulgar, runs from the river up past the Sorbonne to the Luxembourg Gardens. At right angles to it, the Boulevard St Germain stretches, wide and handsome, in a long curve roughly parallel to the river. It has a more serious air than the Boul' Mich, and includes half-way along its length the Place St Germain des Prés, notable equally for its ancient abbey and for two famous cafés almost at its feet. The Deux Magots and the Flore were known after the war as the working place of Sartre and de Beauvoir; now, however delightful, they are famous mainly for being famous.

West from here begins the grand, secretive and aloof seventh *arrondissement*, with its embassies and government offices hidden behind splendid arched gateways. And beyond these again lie the Invalides and the Ecole Militaire, each with its own majestic expanse of grass stretching to the distant Seine.

The Pont des Arts and the Institut de France

St Julien le Pauvre

The Square René Viviani and the Rue de Fürstemberg

Just across the river from Notre-Dame over the Pont au Double is the small Square René Viviani. This pleasantly leafy and shaded place, set back slightly from traffic, contains an ancient false acacia tree, propped up but flourishing. On the day I was there it also contained a fierce park policewoman, stern in her defence of the square's sacrosanct lawns against marauding children. Behind the tree stands a small and even more ancient church, older even than Notre-Dame, named after St Julian the Poor, a medieval bishop called 'the Poor' because he was always giving everything away. Sometimes there are evening concerts in the dark little church; the Romanesque arches and the creamy stone make a sympathetic setting for music. The square itself is a pleasantly quiet place on a sunny morning, with a few tramps and people sitting about reading.

I remember the Rue de Fürstemberg well from my early Paris visits. The shops and streets round it have since moved much upmarket, but the square is as beautiful as ever, especially in winter when you can see through its bare trees to the Rue Jacob beyond. You can't of course see much of the ground-floor architecture now because of the cars. I made this drawing one mild Saturday afternoon in February as people tried desperately to park their Porsches. Behind me, an argument was raging between some policemen and some amiable drunks who denied they'd been begging.

The house and studio of the painter Delacroix are in this square, at No 6. It's interesting to see the considerable style in which a Romantic painter contrived to exist. There are a number of fascinating small rooms; lithographic stones and prints, illustrating Shakespeare; and a big studio in the garden. On one wall is a touching account by his housekeeper of the painter's last days.

The Place Fürstemberg

St Germain des Prés and the Carrefour de Buci

The church of St Germain des Prés is the oldest in Paris, all that is now left of a great Benedictine Abbey. Its Romanesque tower and the small square in front of it are the most striking features of the Boulevard St Germain; they provide a focal point for the life of the Left Bank. Inside, the church is beautiful, dark and mysterious; outside, the square is alive and vivacious. The best and most conspicuous place from which to enjoy the double spectacle is at one of the pavement tables of the Café des Deux Magots. This renowned café is a three-star item on the tourist circuit, but it is still a good place to enjoy watching how smart Parisians meet one another and behave.

Some, however, prefer the marginally calmer Café de Flore almost next door, which has less of a view but more peace. The Flore has very beautiful old cane seats, including some at the side, made to house two affectionate occupants. On a summer evening the pavement in front of it provides a steady stream of entertainment – I've seen fire-eaters, accordionists, flower sellers, flautists, jugglers and a remarkable and extremely mischievous contortionist, who made the polished roofs of the parked cars serve as his stage.

The Carrefour de Buci on a Saturday morning is given over to a market and to the endlessly interesting crowds this attracts. This was where I bought my grapes and tomatoes as a student, and it's not very different now. Later in the day the market shuts up and the pavements are left to the café tables and to the buskers. Off the Boulevard St Germain it's easy to lose one's way among these smaller streets which seem to follow an older plan, running off at unexpected casual angles and ending up near the Seine, behind the Institut de France and the Hôtel des Monnaies. I made this drawing on one of those early spring mornings when, after the February rawness, you suddenly find, to your delight, that it's possible to sit outside again.

Place St Germain des Prés

46

Carrefour de Buci

The Rue Bonaparte

The Faubourg St Germain

The streets of Paris are adorned here and there with imposing gateways, not only magnificent in themselves, but offering glimpses of courtyards and fine mansions. Often these views are, as it were, rationed – available only at the discretion of a *gardien*, to be withdrawn at will from the public gaze behind immense wooden gates. I've always rather liked an overgrown gateway on the Rue Bonaparte, a step or two from the Rue Jacob. This opens onto a handsome courtyard surrounded by creeper-hung houses, occupied now by galleries and the fashion trade. This place looks pleasantly rural, as if the greenery were growing on the walls of a quiet but comfortable provincial hotel, an impression which survives despite the metal business plaques and the scent poster. Further west, where the

Boulevard St Germain begins to curve back towards the river, are the more severely official façades of the great ministries on the Rue de Grenelle and the Rue de Varenne. These are stately and classical, and all are symmetrical, so that gazing in through the centre of the gateway one has the feeling of standing on a meridian. But despite the Greek and Roman derivation of their architectural motifs they have all ended up looking extremely French – not unlike the labels on bottles of Bordeaux. I particularly like those where instead of a triangular pediment there is a rounded one – shallow and elliptical as in the gateway to Marshal Foch's mansion on the Rue de Varenne, or full and semicircular like that in the centre of the Hôtel des Invalides (pages 60–61). All the same, for all their

grandeur, these official streets of the seventh *arrondissement* have less life on them than those of the Left Bank in general: more dispatch riders, navy-blue uniforms and tricolours and an air of diligence and importance, of weight rather than vivacity.

One curious and beautiful surprise on the Rue de Grenelle is the Fontaine des Quatre Saisons. This fountain was built (in 1739–45) because, magnificent or not, the Faubourg had no water. At the top of it, Paris looks down on the Seine and the Marne. Though it's tempting to smile at such innocent personifications, it's also pleasant in these dry metropolitan streets to be even momentarily reminded of wider horizons and of the great rivers that gave the city life and beauty.

Foch's house in the Rue de Grenelle

Façades on the Rue de Grenelle and the Rue de Varenne   Fontaine des Quatre Saisons

The Rue Maître Albert and the Jardin des Plantes

From a fifth-floor hotel room high up in the Rue Maître Albert one can look down into this quiet street as if into a deep canyon, watch the people walking in it and see at the far end the traffic on the Quai de la Tournelle. The Rue Maître Albert is one of the more easterly of the many small streets and alleys that run up from the Seine quays towards the Boulevard St Germain, streets that are sometimes mere crevices between precipitous and overhanging cliffs of old houses. Many of these streets are thronged with tourists, and at street level most are full of small restaurants and fast-food shops.

If one follows the Seine east from here, past the Ile St Louis, one comes after about a kilometre to the Jardin des Plantes, a beautiful and restoring place and, for some reason, quieter than the other big Parisian gardens. Compared with, say, Kew Gardens, its layout is extremely formal. Two long straight avenues of planes, trimmed and clipped to almost geometrical precision, stretch away from the river and the Place Valhubert up the rising ground towards the central museum building and the Mosque. Whether in full summer foliage or bare and wintry, I love these magnificent avenues: the slight upward curve of the slope stops the perspective from being too rigidly mechanical, and the very Parisian sensation of trained and controlled natural growth is agreeable.

The avenues are separated and flanked by areas of neat bushes and bordered flowerbeds, like a large-scale version of the Chelsea Physic Garden. In the morning especially, people come here to jog or to do exercises; in the afternoons there are families and prams. As in other Parisian public gardens, a sense of decorum is maintained, or maybe just comes naturally; perhaps it is because there are no lawns to lie about on. There is instead an air of botanical dedication with statues of Buffon and Lamarck. The hothouse or Jardin d'Hiver, more heavily built than the Kew Gardens greenhouses, is filled with a Douanier Rousseauesque profusion of plants, and with streams and a concrete grotto. The western corner of the Jardin des Plantes is more romantically and informally laid out than the main garden, with a knoll and a big cedar tree.

The Rue Maître Albert

50

The Allée Buffon in the Jardin des Plantes

The Fontaine de Médicis

Palais du Luxembourg

The Fontaine de Médicis

The Fontaine de Médicis is a seductive Parisian combination of formal sculpture, water, trees, and people. On a warm day it offers the prospect of relaxed and sustained indolence, of peacefulness broken only by the trickle of water and the beating of pigeons' wings. The fountain itself is Italian in manner and dates from the 1620s, but the white figures of Acis and Galatea about to be attacked by Polyphemus are mid-nineteenth-century. It stands to the east of the Luxembourg Palace at the end of a long rectangular basin, secluded from the rest of the gardens by trees and formal shrubs: the paths round it are thick with the simple, all-purpose and durable metal chairs which are such a pleasant and useful feature of the Paris parks. They are often used in pairs: one for sitting or dozing on, the other for putting your feet up. The activities in these idyllic surroundings on a summer afternoon are reading the paper, conversation, study, letter-reading and writing, and prolonged flirtations.

The Luxembourg Palace itself is a handsome, wide building, facing an octagonal boating pool. Here, as in the Tuileries Gardens, children hire home-made sailing boats by the hour from an attendant with a boat-trolley.

The most spectacular feature of the Luxembourg Gardens is the prospect south from the palace towards the Observatoire (see overleaf). Its straightness and length are underlined by the parallel alleys of clipped chestnuts, in places almost converging overhead, which draw the eye onwards.

This part of the gardens was laid out in the grounds of a monastery demolished in the Revolution. It is beautiful and peaceful, its clean lawns preserved from intruders except for the one which is set aside for children to play on.

Fontaine de Médicis

The Luxembourg Gardens

The Luxembourg Gardens in summer and autumn

Whenever it is warm enough to sit outside, chess players gather in that north-eastern corner of the Luxembourg Gardens nearest to Saint Sulpice. Sometimes they are accompanied by what look like loyal but long-suffering partners, some following the games with close interest, others merely waiting. On a really hot day, the chess takes on the superficial appearance of a game for the beach. But it's clearly more serious than that. The layout is standard: two seats for sitting on, two for supporting the board and the two clocks which are struck each time someone makes a move. The most expert games attract small groups of onlookers, silent and rapt. Draughts and cards are also played here, but without the same following: it's the chess that draws the crowds.

The long chestnut alleys leading towards the Observatoire, the Jardin Robert Cavelier-de-la-Salle and the Jardin Marco Polo, are also filled with activity. Children play ping-pong on the concrete tables built for them, smaller children make tunnels for themselves by putting rows of the metal chairs side by side and crawling through them; grown-ups do callisthenics individually, and practise T'ai Chi in small and well-disciplined groups.

I like the gardens in winter, when the trees are black, the kiosks have closed up, neat piles of sawn-up logs lie about under the trees, and well-muffled-up children take rides in the donkey carts. But I like them best of all in autumn, as the chestnuts change colour, some slightly out of sync, yellower or browner than the others. Then the fallen leaves hide the alley sand and the ground is the same colour as the walls of foliage, people begin to walk in the gardens in warmer clothes, and the statues begin to look chilly and inadequately clad.

chess players in the Luxembourg Gardens

Chestnuts in the Luxembourg Gardens, October

The Rue Mouffetard

The Rue Mouffetard

It is hard to know exactly how it is that on
one occasion a place can seem curious,
interesting and genuine, and yet on another
can strike one as spoilt: too picturesque,
over the top, a bit vulgar. I first saw the Rue
Mouffetard on a February evening and
thought it, though pretty, overly done-up –
too many small restaurants and a general
air of self-conscious and commercial
tarting-up. But the next morning, when I
made these drawings, it all looked real
enough, and timeless; the houses which
overhang the narrow street of market
stalls could have come straight out of *Les
Enfants du Paradis*. Many of the younger
stallholders looked more like actors than
shopkeepers; the group of four boys
selling daffodils were Saturday amateurs,
and a bit sheepish about it. It was rainy
at first and the canopies gave the stalls,
especially in the even narrower side-

streets, the flavour of a Moroccan souk.
The street gradually became crowded with
perfectly genuine Saturday morning
shoppers, entertained by various musicians
– a trumpeter with a pig, a barrel organist
with a monkey, a small jazz group down
at the bottom of the street – so that the
picturesqueness got submerged in the
serious spectacle of buying the weekend
food. People doing the shopping make
good subjects, for – like racegoers or people
watching cricket – they are too intent on
the matter in hand to notice, let alone mind,
that anyone is drawing them.

Degas was dismissive of drawing in the
open, which he once described as an open-air
sport. Drawing on the streets needs some
determination: people find the process
interesting to watch, ask the way or the
time, discuss their own drawings and
techniques, or just tiptoe up silently to peep

at what one is doing. However resolutely
I may try to ignore this, it still breaks my
concentration and puts me off; the uneasy
sense of being watched, scrutinised, persists
long after the onlooker has got bored and
crept away. But often these encounters have
been interesting, occasionally delightful,
all part of the experience of drawing on the
spot.

It is worth trying to be as comfortable as
you can. It is possible to stand and draw
holding a sketchbook or a board, but only
for a while; as soon as you begin to think
more about the discomfort than the subject,
the drawing is done for. An easel is useful
if you already know where you are going, but
it's a nuisance to cart around if you are just
looking. A sketching stool is better, though
it gives you a low-level viewpoint; or you can
use a flat bit of wall – a parapet, for instance
– as a sort of drawing desk, or seat.

The Rue Mouffetard

The Hôtel des Invalides

The Hôtel des Invalides

The Invalides was built in 1671–6 to provide accommodation for up to 4,000 old soldiers who had been invalided out and who would otherwise have been reduced to beggary, a conspicuous and embarrassing reminder of the realities of war. The approach from the river is magnificent. At first, seen from a distance, the building is dominated by the splendid gilded dome over the chapel. But as you walk up the grassy Esplanade, the fine façade by Libéral Bruant asserts itself more and more until by the time you reach the gates of the garden, where the drawing was made, the dome has disappeared and you can see the noble frontage undistracted by anything beyond. Everything about the Invalides glorifies seventeenth-century militarism – the trophies round the roof windows, the picturesque batteries of bronze cannon at the edge of the fortified moat, and the monumental arched doorway over which rides Louis XIV supported by Prudence and Justice. Even the clipped yews look like rows of toy soldiers.

Val-de-Grâce and St Sulpice

The magnificent church of Val-de-Grâce was built in thanks for the birth, in 1638, of Louis XIV. Its splendidly sure-footed unity of style survived despite a change of architect: from Mansart to Lemercier.

The same cannot be said of the front of St Sulpice, which looks down onto a pretty marble fountain in the middle of a quiet square. The church with its two-tiered colonnades is impressive but there is something odd about it. When it was rebuilt in the eighteenth century to a design by the Italian architect Servandoni, his ideas were modified or abandoned by the locals, so that instead of being a work of monumental grandeur the façade is something of a hotch-potch. Its inkwell towers do not quite match one another: once one has noticed this, its out-of-kilter skyline, poking up out of the Left Bank roofs or above the Luxembourg Gardens, is unmistakable.

The Val-de-Grâce from the Place A. Laveran

St Sulpice and the Fontaine des Quatre Points Cardinaux

The Place de la Contrescarpe and the Tour Montparnasse

Familiar Parisian scenes are changing inexorably and in oddly different ways. In the Place de la Contrescarpe all the transformations have occurred at ground level – just as they do in an English High Street where the ground-floor shops are periodically ripped out and replaced, but the two or three upper storeys – not five or more as in Paris – remain untouched. If one were to blot out this Parisian ground floor the huddle of buildings would seem in all essentials untouched since the eighteenth century.

64

The Place de la Contrescarpe

The Tour montparnasse

By contrast, in the Place du 18 Juin 1940 in front of the Montparnasse terminus, the structure of the old corner bar is unaltered up as far as the sky sign. But the feel of the whole area was changed once and for all by the arrival in 1973 of the city's first new skyscraper, the Tour Montparnasse, and by the brash and temporary-looking shopping complex round its skirts. The tower is still the only tall building for miles. From the top you get a good view down onto the surviving layout of streets and boulevards, with all the ant-like activity of the new Left Bank at your feet, half planned, half accidental. The tower itself could be thought an arrogant intrusion; but so could the Eiffel Tower.

The Place du Parvis Notre-Dame

The Islands and the Marais

Of the original group of islands and islets in the Seine, the Ile de la Cité was the biggest and the first to be inhabited – by the Parisii, who called it Lutetia. It was invaded by the Romans and became the heart of growing Paris. But even though its shore was fortified, the Ile de la Cité remained in parts fragmented. Its western, downstream tip crumbled away into a sort of archipelago of muddy islets until it was taken in hand and tidied up in the late sixteenth century, just before the Pont Neuf was built. Although its most celebrated feature and in touristic terms its most tempting honey-pot is still Notre-Dame, with the Sainte-Chapelle a beautiful but secondary treasure, most of the Ile de la Cité that one sees today is nineteenth century and post-Haussmann. It is composed, what is more, of impersonal and forbidding institutions: the criminal and commercial law-courts, the perfecture of police, the Conciergerie, the big Hôtel-Dieu hospital. Its most familiar sights may be the vast crowds photographing the façade of Notre-Dame from the Parvis in front of it, and the long lines of tour coaches disgorging or re-ingesting their weary cargoes at its rear end, but its most characteristic sounds are the wailing police sirens heralding a grey convoy of vanloads of policemen and prisoners.

Just upstream from the Cité were two much smaller marshy islands, the Ile Notre-Dame and the Ile aux Vaches. These were only united in the early seventeenth century by the joint efforts of two financiers and an astute contractor, Marie (of the Pont Marie). In return for building two stone (that is to say, substantial) bridges to connect the new Ile St Louis with the left and right banks, Louis XIII allowed this formidable trio to sell off the new island's land for building. This proved to be a well-thought-out arrangement whereby the Ile St Louis acquired both its handsome and uniformly classical architecture and its very logical ground-plan: the island is bisected by a single long, straight street, the Rue St Louis en l'Ile, at right angles to which run seven short but equally straight side-streets. The whole island is encircled by an almost continuous quay, tranquil, tree-shaded and of great beauty. Indeed, after the Ile de la Cité, the Ile St Louis seems a quiet and peaceful backwater, though now – as was intended when it was built – it is clearly substantial, comfortable, and rich.

The Marais or Marsh lies just across the river to the north, and its development dates largely from about the same time as that of the Ile St Louis. But the Place des Vosges, its central and grandest feature which sparked off the rest of the building work, was begun by Henri IV two decades earlier, in 1605. The Marais soon included many of the city's finest and most impressive mansions.

But after the Revolution, having been deprived by the Terror of its original aristocratic inhabitants, the Marais became run down, neglected, and generally the worse for wear. In place of the noblemen were installed the merchants, craftsmen and tradesmen who gave the area its uniquely cosmopolitan and polyglot vitality and who still in some part remain. But recently, while Malraux was Minister of Culture, the Marais was rehabilitated and it is once again becoming smart and wealthy. The workshops are giving way to antique dealers, the bistros are getting more expensive and the whole Marais is experiencing in varying degrees a visible and inexorable drift upmarket – something which is turning out to be a very mixed blessing.

The Palais de Justice: the Salle des Pas Perdus

The Ile de la Cité

This is not one of my favourite parts of Paris.
Much of the Ile de la Cité is given over to
institutions: the Church, the Law, the Police,
Medicine. The rest has been taken over by
tourism, whose parked coaches fill the
streets at the back of Notre-Dame and
provide a garish foreground to the views
of its apse, its remarkable flying buttresses,
and the houses that surround it. At the
western end of Notre-Dame, the Place du
Parvis is an open, traffic-free space in front
of the much-photographed façade of the
cathedral. Beyond the *place* are the police
headquarters and the law-courts, the Palais
de Justice. Anyone can go in. The majesty
of the law is not played down in its great
halls and corridors. But the lawyers do not
wear wigs and look in consequence very
much like ordinary people, with gowns
instead of coats, papers and briefcases
instead of the shopping, but otherwise

much the same as the rest of us. Perhaps
this should not seem surprising, but
somehow, amidst all the polished marble
pomp and grandeur, it does.

But the island has its delights too. Almost
on the doorstep of the Palais de Justice,
by the Cité Métro station, is the Sunday
bird market. This is always worth a visit.
The birds are strange and pretty, but not
half as fascinating as the people buying
and selling them: one I drew had set off
early in the morning with a great lorryload
of tiny birds from a base far out of Paris.
Yet it's the *life*, the whole occasion, that
makes the bird market interesting – not the
setting. The places on the island that I like
best for themselves are the Place Dauphine,
a handsome chestnut-filled triangle at the
western end, and still further west the
pretty Square du Vert Galant at its tip,
a relaxed and unofficial place.

The Place Louis Lépine: the bird market

The Quai de l'Archevêché

The Ile St Louis

The Pont Louis-Philippe connects the Ile St Louis with the Right Bank at the western end of the Marais. Beyond it is the much older and prettier Pont Marie. The Quai de Bourbon here is pleasantly shabby; it has not yet been done up, as have many of the other quaysides of central Paris. Its stones are uneven and worn, and in September, the surface sloping into the water is still green with self-sown weeds. This particular stretch of quayside has few benches, but people sit and picnic on the wide raised pavement beneath the bridge. It all has an agreeably accidental air, which the recently refurbished quaysides, for all their carefully designed ramps, terraces and angled surfaces, have inevitably lost – for the time being at least. Like quaysides in general, it also has a faintly disreputable air: quite an asset on the Ile St Louis, which tends to be over-genteel.

The Rue St Louis en l'Ile runs the length of the island, providing one of the city's most notable long, straight perspectives. (Another is the Rue Jacob/Rue de l'Université on the Left Bank.) At this eastern end it is rather grand: the chestnuts to the right of the drawing are in the garden of the Hôtel Lambert, built – like the church of St Louis en l'Ile, whose pierced spire can be seen further down the street – by Le Vau, who lived on the island. Beyond the church, the street becomes a bit more commercial in a gentrified sort of way – Salons de Thé rather than plain cafés, and gift shops. But these are the inevitable trappings of any district enriched by visitors, and can't be helped.

The quays that surround the island have big trees growing up either from street level or from the quay below, but the straight streets through the island are too narrow for trees. The lack of them emphasises the severity of the grid on which the island was planned. In contrast there are fine trees in the Square Barye, the pointed and terraced south-western tip of the island, which echoes the Square du Vert Galant at the far end of the Ile de la Cité but is presently much shabbier.

While at work on these drawings, I began to notice and admire the familiar Parisian metal lamp-standard, solid, rounded and helmet-like at the top, and almost as characteristic an element on the city's pavements as the Morris column (for posters) or the Wallace drinking fountain.

The Quai de Bourbon and the Pont Louis-Philippe

The Rue St Louis en l'Ile

The houses of the Ile St Louis

In summer the surrounding foliage screens and secludes the island's houses from the river and one hardly pays any attention to them. But in winter it's easy to see the handsome frontage which the Ile St Louis then presents to the outer world. The finest and the oldest is to be seen along the Quai de Bourbon and the Quai d'Anjou on the northern side. Here there are beautiful groupings of tall houses, their stone façades giving or undulating slightly with time, the whole effect one of general, but not rigid,

symmetry. As usual, they are tall: five storeys and another in the roof; and they have big arched entrances, sometimes opening into an inner courtyard of considerable splendour. One could do worse than live in one of those rooms, with a view of the river and its fascinating traffic.

Even the short streets that cut through the island from side to side – the Rue Le Regrattier, the Rue des Deux Ponts, the Rue Poulletier – seem deep and narrow, hardly more than slits, and are further

narrowed at pavement level by the inevitable line of parked cars.

One of the most beautiful and striking views of the island is of its pointed western tip. Looking at it from the opposite bank of the river one can see clearly the different layers of the island: the low tree-lined quayside; the road built up on a terrace above it; the tall houses rising above the foliage, and adding here and there a little of their own by virtue of their roof gardens.

72

The western tip of the Ile St Louis

The Rue Le Regrattier

The Ile St Louis: The Quai de Bourbon and the Quai de Béthune

The detailing of the great dark houses of the north-facing Quai de Bourbon and the Quai d'Anjou is interesting for the beautiful seventeenth-century woodwork and stonework but also for the pleasant glimpses of domesticity they offer. Whether seen in close-up or from a distance, the repeating patterns and delicate horizontal lines of their white-painted shutters are an important element here as on many typical Parisian façades.

The houses along the Quai de Béthune on the other side of the island, the side facing the Left Bank, are less interesting architecturally, but beautiful all the same when the sun lights up their white walls behind the tracery of bare branches. In spring the acacias here are the last trees to come out, still bare when the foliage of chestnuts and planes is far advanced, and this gives a prolonged wintry feeling to this stretch of riverside. There is no quayside beneath the roadway of the Quai de Béthune, so everyone walks along this pavement. I like the small round arch at the side of the Pont de la Tournelle, though the whole bridge gives the impression of being made up of parts that don't quite match. From the bridge itself there are good views of the Ile de la Cité and the back of Notre-Dame, and a distant view upstream towards the new metal-and-glass offices gleaming along the Port de la Rapée, and the big chimneys beyond them. This is a view that somehow seems to belong to a different city altogether, booming yet provincial.

Doorway on the Quai de Bourbon

The Quai de Béthune

St Paul-St Louis and the Horses of Apollo

Whereas the domestic Ile St Louis is all more or less of a piece, the commercial Marais is remarkably diverse, with extremes of elegance and shabbiness, activity and repose. Its main artery is the eastern end of the ramrod-straight Rue de Rivoli and its curving continuation, the older and far more beautiful Rue St Antoine. The older street is just as wide, but more supple, weaving slightly to and fro as it makes its way to the Place de la Bastille, and thus showing off its tall creamy-grey houses to good effect. The main architectural landmark of its southern side is the church of St Paul-St Louis, an imposing structure built by the Jesuits between 1626 and 1641. It embodies an odd paradox, for its large dome – a Jesuit innovation – is tucked away behind the flamboyant frontage so that from close at hand one hardly notices it. I enjoy this façade for the exuberant, child-like enthusiasm with which the classical splendour has been piled on, as if round an old-fashioned steam organ at a fairground. It holds its own powerfully against the foreground of teeming traffic and scurrying pedestrians – a scene whose details may have changed but whose essentials still remain after 350 years.

It would be hard to miss St Paul-St Louis.

But not all the treasures of the Marais are so conspicuous. You have to go and look for the slendid Horses of Apollo, in the courtyard of the Hôtel de Rohan. This bas-relief of the early eighteenth century is surprisingly alive, vivid and airy: it looks almost as if it had been painted with stone. On the afternoon I was there, all was quiet: only a few visitors came in to look at this haunting and poetic evocation of horses slaking their thirst. The present-day equivalent, filling up at a petrol station, is interesting too, but it's harder to be touched by this newer kind of horse-power.

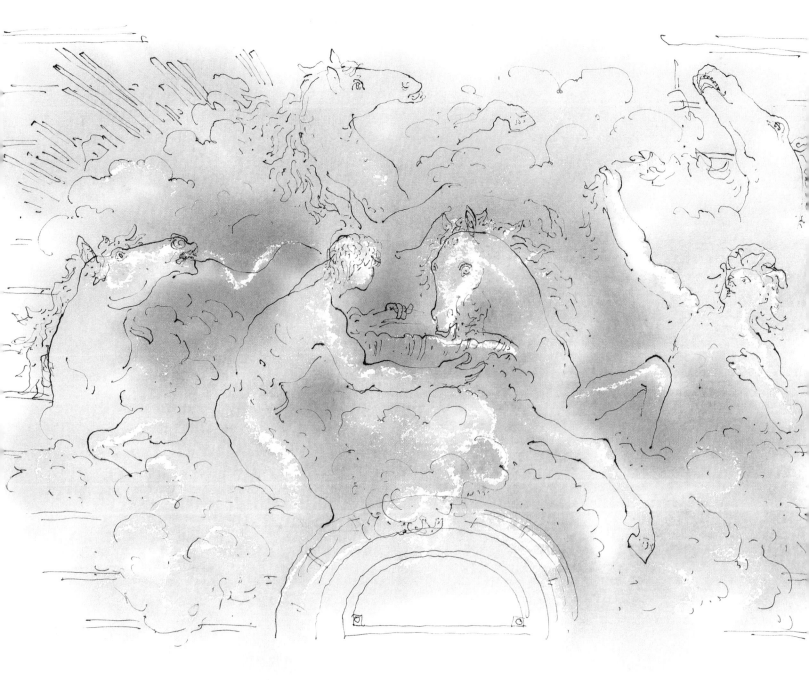

The Hôtel de Rohan - the Horses of Apollo

The Rue St Antoine and the church of St Paul-St Louis

The Rue St Antoine : the façade of the Hôtel Sully

The Hôtel Sully

Half-way along the Rue St Antoine between
St Paul-St Louis and the Place de la Bastille
is a fine symmetrical façade in weathered
yellowish-grey stone, its two wings flanking
a central arch. Through this one can enter a
Renaissance courtyard of great beauty, its
walls embellished with sculptured figures.
The Hôtel Sully is grand, but somehow not
overbearing: one feels enhanced, not reduced
to insignificance, by the scale and by all the
carefully worked-out classical detail and
ornament around one. The place is also put
to good use: not only as the headquarters
of the Monuments Historiques et Sites, but

also for music and open-air theatre. I saw
here an impassioned open-air theatrical
performance about the Revolution in its
bicentenary year, and also drew here to the
sound of an Aeolian harp – a pleasant if slightly
over-the-top experience on a warm evening.
I had to throw the drawing away.

In the farthest wall of this courtyard,
between two sphinxes, is another door
leading into a second courtyard with
parterres, less like a stone room and more
like a walled garden. And from this, one
can go through yet a third door and find
oneself in the arcade surrounding the great

Place des Vosges. This square has a great
attraction for lively parties of visiting
schoolchildren – many of them from other
countries – to picnic, an activity which gives
the place not only a pleasant vitality, but also
a feeling of being well used. I drew several
of these groups, composed of delightful and
inquisitive children under the wing of their
friendly teachers.

The long, dark arcades of the Place des
Vosges (see page 82) remind me of those
in northern Italian towns like Padua or
Siena, with their beautiful repeating
patterns of light and shade. Wherever one

78

The courtyard of the Hôtel Sully

Lunchtime in the Place des Vosges

enters the square, at either of its two
northern corners, or through the central
arches in its north and south sides, it is always
a startling architectural experience – of
planning and determined execution
certainly, but also of grace and pleasure.
The arcades are busy now, with restaurants
and cafés and with prosperous-looking
antiquaires, while outside on the pavement
are the more temporary stalls of jewellery
makers and other craftsmen. There are street
musicians too, and often a film crew or the
surprisingly complicated team needed to
set up a fashion photograph.

The Place des Vosges

At the beginning of the seventeenth century, Henri IV ordered the creation of two fine public spaces – the triangular Place Dauphine and the square Place des Vosges. This last is, with the Place de la Concorde, the most magnificent formal open space in Paris. It is surrounded by the uniformly patterned elevations of thirty-six mansions. Two of these, the Pavillon de la Reine in the centre of this drawing and the Pavillon du Roi facing it across the square, form centre-pieces for the north and south sides and are suitably bigger than all the other houses, but the overall unity of scale is preserved. At ground level an unbroken arcade runs round the whole square, while underneath the arches there are café tables, restaurants, musicians and pedlars, and a constant flow of leisurely visitors. The square itself is formally laid out with grass, sand, trees, and fountains, and is a good place to sit and take stock.

The Place des Vosges was meant to be splendid and to form the nucleus of the newly developing Marais, and it succeeded triumphantly. It is a notable example of Parisian planning at its best – grand but human, intended for occupation and not yet primarily for glorification. In this it was the precursor of and inspiration for Inigo Jones's Piazza in Covent Garden, and for the later formal set-pieces of eighteenth-century Bath.

The early prints of the Place des Vosges show only the buildings. The great clump of chestnuts in the middle of the square was planted just before the Revolution, the smaller surrounding limes much later: the trees give shade and freshness, though they prevent one from seeing the *place* in its entirety. But if one stands in winter at the edge of the central clump looking out, one can feel the grandeur of the original conception without any intervening foliage to distract the visitor's eye.

The north side of the Place des Vosges

Porte de Clisson

maison de Jacques Coeur

Rue Vieille du Temple

Rue des Rosiers

The Place des Vosges and the Marais streets

While the Place des Vosges is the most spectacular of the set pieces of the Marais, the surrounding streets, too, are stuffed with curious and beautiful buildings: the most important of them well looked-after, though some of the others are still in a state of quite theatrical dilapidation. On the Rue des Archives stands the Porte de Clisson, looking exactly like a castle gatehouse in a medieval miniature. It is the only remnant left standing of the ancient fourteenth-century manor house of Olivier de Clisson, Constable of France. A little way down the street, opposite the Rue du Plâtre, is the fifteenth-century house of Jacques Cœur, its handsome façade patterned both by its solid white stonework and by the diaper designs in the brickwork. It's not so eye-catching as the fairy-tale Porte de Clisson, but it is notable as one of the city's oldest houses, solidly built and durable.

Many of the older Marais houses are hidden behind imposing gateways. The finest and most curious, that of the Hôtel des Ambassadeurs de Hollande in the Rue Vieille du Temple, is a splendid concoction of allegorical stone figures and cherubs and Medusas' heads in carved wood. It was here that, in 1776, Beaumarchais wrote *The Marriage of Figaro*.

The Tour St Jacques and the church of St Gervais-St Protais

In the Square de la Tour St Jacques, west of the Hôtel de Ville, stands one of the prominent features of the central Paris skyline – the Tour St Jacques, originally the belfry of a church now long vanished, but later used as a shot-tower. I like the spiky-looking, grotesque figures at its top corners, and the time-worn stone lion that sits like a drowsy cat near its base. The square is pleasantly shaded and, if not exactly peaceful – the Rue de Rivoli runs along its north side – at least it offers benches and greenery. In the early evenings a soup kitchen parks on the south side, in the Avenue Victoria, and distributes food in cardboard boxes to the needy who have gathered there to wait for it. For a time, the benches are occupied by these grown-up picnickers, who eat and chat for a while and then disperse one by one into the evening.

The Tour St Jacques

To the east of the Hôtel de Ville stands another conspicuous church tower, this one still a going concern. St Gervais-St Protais reminds me, with its slate and tile roofs, of a large provincial church; the streets behind it also have a provincial air, being old, huddled together and rather quiet – penetrable by bike but not by car. There are old wooden houses here that almost meet across narrow alleys, and passageways and courts that slope steeply down towards the river. This really *is* a backwater – secluded, passed by, given over to the sale of religious books, and to a hostel for young people: a far cry from the vitality and the turmoil of the true Marais. Couperin was the organist of the church, and lived nearby in the Rue François Miron.

St Gervais - St Protais

The Cour Carrée

The Pyramid

The Arc de Triomphe du Carrousel

The Obélisque and the Marly Horses

The Arc de Triomphe

The Grande Arche

The Grand Alignment

Parisian single-mindedness and the determination to impress are seen at their most awesome in the remorseless alignment that begins at the Palais du Louvre and runs through its courtyards, past the Carrousel arch, through the Tuileries Gardens, across the Place de la Concorde, and up the long Champs-Elysées to the distant Arc de Triomphe at the top of the rise. The same line then continues on, though by now out of sight, past the Porte Maillot and the Pont de Neuilly to the Grande Arche at La Défense. It's impressive, certainly; but a long straight line is pretty boring, no use for anything but grand parades and speeding traffic: not much point. The inspired feature of this great alignment is that it's cunningly broken up: at each stage some further landmark catches one's eye and makes one curious, spurs one on and then, as one nears it, reveals yet another eye-catching device to provide a still further goal. From the courtyard of the Cour Carrée in the Palais du Louvre one can already see through a classical arched doorway the gleaming new Pyramid. Through the glass sides of the Pyramid one sees the Carrousel arch. Through the Carrousel's central arch one sees the Obelisk at the centre of the Place de la Concorde and, even beyond this, the Marly Horses and the Champs-Elysées and on up to Napoleon's Arc de Triomphe. One has to continue right up to this and stand beneath it to grasp the visual progression onwards to the Grande Arche at La Défense, but once one's done this it's as firmly fixed in the imagination, as much part of the whole experience, as if the ground were flat and it could all be taken in at a single glance. This succession of Parisian landmarks set out all in a row is remarkable: it's as if one could stand on the steps of the British Museum and see, all on the same axis, across Trafalgar Square and through Marble Arch to Cleopatra's Needle, the Cenotaph and the Hyde Park Corner Quadriga, on through the Decimus Burton screen to the Albert Memorial, the Lloyds building and Canary Wharf.

In the Parisian arrangement there are however two flaws, one minor, one major. The first is a slight change of direction, very skilfully disguised. The Louvre is not in fact on quite the same axis as all the rest; but the two intersect at the Carrousel arch, which has been flanked with chestnuts so that looking west one barely notices any inconsistency. The more serious drawback concerns the Grande Arche at La Défense. From a distance, the whole idea looks new, splendid, and arresting – stupendous, even. But after one has plodded up to the arch itself and peeped ant-like through it at the view beyond, one is overcome with an overwhelming sense of disappointment, of vacuum. One's eye takes in not some appropriate visual climax but a suburban cemetery, some dreary expressway embankments and some hideous old tower-block flats that look like camouflaged but abandoned military installations. Looking through the Grande Arche is like that other contemporary experience, looking at a television set with a blank screen. Maybe in due course an appropriate picture will appear. But for the present it's impossible not to ask if the effort was all really worth it: is this architecture or just bombast?

The Cour Carrée of the Louvre

As you enter the Louvre from the Place du Louvre, crossing the old moat and going through an archway, you find yourself in this square enclosed courtyard, the Cour Carrée, facing the Clock Pavilion. By now your head may be swimming with vast elevations, enormous columns and incrustations of sculpture; even so, this particular section of Renaissance wall is clearly a cut above the others. It is the oldest portion of the Cour Carrée and the most distinguished: it was built by Pierre Lescot and the graceful sculptures are by Jean Goujon. In the sixteenth century, this decorous-looking Cour Carrée was the scene of bear- and lion-baiting, and it was here that, in 1572, during the Massacre of St Bartholomew, the Protestants of the Court were murdered.

Today one automatically thinks of the Louvre as an art gallery and museum, but of course it began as a fortress. It was built by Philippe Auguste – the foundations can be seen as you enter it from the Pyramid. It was only later that it became a palace, built and rebuilt, refurbished and then turned over to a curious hotch-potch of inhabitants when Louis XIV abandoned it in favour of Versailles. The western part of it was burnt down in the Commune.

Much of the interest and vitality of the Cour Carrée now comes from the eager if bemused crowds from many countries, who cross it on their way to the Pyramid.

The Cour Carrée and the Clock Pavilion

90   The Pei Pyramid and the Pavillon de Flore

The Louvre: The Cour Napoléon III and the Pyramid

Where the Cour Napoléon III widens out into the Jardin du Carrousel, it's tempting to think of its pavilions as merely inspired hunks of stage scenery, or as two great cliffs or headlands flanking the view of the Tuileries Gardens beyond it. But this was never their original purpose, for the view westwards (to the right of the drawing) was until 1871 shut off by Catherine de Médicis' Palais des Tuileries. It is thanks to the Communards, who in 1871 set fire to this palace and completely destroyed it, that one can now see through the Carrousel arch to the trees and parterres of the Tuileries stretching away beyond it.

The skyline of this end of the Louvre is dominated by the grandiose additions, from 1852 onwards, designed for Napoleon III by Visconti, the architect of the tomb of Napoleon I. But by far the most striking feature of the Cour Napoléon III is the new steel-and-glass pyramid by Ieoh Ming Pei, opened in 1989. Some think this a brash and irreverent intrusion into a sacrosanct and historic place. I don't share this view. The Visconti masonry heaped around it was itself in its own time raw and intrusive, and on a colossal scale: Pei's elegant little pyramid is, if anything, rather dwarfed by its grand setting. The pyramid even looks

slightly temporary, as if it could, if need arose, be towed away. But as a splendid ticket office and foyer, it seems a perfectly appropriate symbol of the Louvre's present role as a museum. Inevitably it looks much more transparent from the inside looking out than when you are looking from outside through two walls of dusty glass at the view beyond. But flanked by Napoleon III's flamboyant and rather pushy extensions, and especially when the new fountains are playing in their beautifully engineered and geometrical pools, the Pyramid is an unforgettable addition to the sights of Paris.

The central alley looking west

The Tuileries Gardens

The gardens of the Tuileries epitomise the Parisian way of organising a public space. Orderly, even rigid in conception, and geometrically planned, there is no touch here of the accidental or the informal. The surface is mainly of hard sand and the ornaments are either useful and practical – benches, shelters, litter-bins, refreshments kiosks – or formally arranged sculpture, including some characteristic works by Maillol which now impart their own flavour to the surroundings. As you walk through the gardens, you can enjoy the changing perspectives of the lines of tree trunks. In summer the foliage is thick and heavy and makes it a pleasant shady place to walk, but the formality of the design is most obvious when the trees are bare (see page 6) and one can see the pattern of trunks and branches black against sand and sky.

The Tuileries were originally an area of clay used for making tiles, hence the name.

The place was also – like the Buttes Chaumont and many other Parisian public spaces – once used as a rubbish tip or dump. It was first laid out as a park in the sixteenth century, for Catherine de Médicis, but reshaped a century later by the gardener Le Nôtre as a formal open-air extension of the Louvre palace. His raised terraces still screen it from the Rue de Rivoli and from the Seine. On the more northerly of these terraces stands the Jeu de Paume museum, presently being rebuilt; on the southern, nearer the river, stands the Orangerie with its Impressionist collection. The western ends of these terraces overlook the Place de la Concorde and offer magnificent prospects of its pavilions, of the Champs-Elysées, and of the Grand Palais rising up above its surrounding chestnuts.

The Tuileries are separated from the Louvre's Cour Napoléon III and the Pyramid by the Jardin du Carrousel, the squarish

area between the two farthest wings of the Louvre. It is normally dominated by its pretty – if lightweight – triumphal arch which has been described as a delightful garden ornament. But when I drew it the garden had been transformed by the vast excavations necessary for completing the work on the Louvre. Here one sees laid open the layers of bluish and yellow clay, the foundations of the burnt-down Palais des Tuileries, and on the right a semicircular outer bastion of the original fortress. I would have liked to make a head-on drawing of the arch, but from the front it's all firmly screened from view. However, you can look through the wire netting at the side at this astonishing vision of an older, long forgotten, Paris. This view is given scale by the one or two ant-like archaeologists sitting at their trestle table or prodding away at the stones and the clay, bare-legged in shorts in the autumn sun, like children on the beach.

The Tuileries Gardens: the Orangerie

The Carrousel arch

The Winged Horses of the Tuileries

The Winged Horses, by the sculptor Coysevox, stand at the western end of the central alley of the gardens, overlooking the Place de la Concorde. One supports Mercury, the other Fame. I find both the sculptures and indeed the whole prospect endlessly exhilarating, whatever the weather – the horses look just as good when silhouetted dark against a cloudy or sunset sky as when one sees them glowing in the morning sunlight. Two more white horses, by Coustou, with splendidly flowing manes but wingless, rear up as if at the traffic, at the far side of the Place. Confusingly, these are known as the Marly Horses, though the Winged Horses, too, came from the Château of Marly. The movement, confidence and flamboyance of all four represent for me the most seductive aspects of French seventeenth-century sculpture. The Marly Horses are more prominently placed and better known but you have to look up at them amid the rush of vehicles, whereas from the terrace behind the Winged Horses you can look down on the maelstrom of the Place de la Concorde with a certain detachment, or – like Mercury – turn your back on it entirely.

Mercury on a Winged Horse and the Place de la Concorde

The Place de la Concorde

Like the Louvre, the Place de la Concorde took a long time to achieve its present state. It was begun in 1755 by the architect Gabriel with the creation of the eight fine pavilions and the magnificent façades of what are now the Hôtel Crillon and the Hôtel de la Marine. During the Revolution the guillotine was set up in the Place, at first in front of the Crillon and then near the gateway into the Tuileries. The impersonal obelisk was chosen in the politically insecure 1830s for its bland neutrality: no one would

be likely to pull it down, as they would the statue of a discarded ruler. The fountains and the statues, each representing a French town, were added in the reign of Louis-Philippe under the direction of Hittorff, the ingenious architect of the Gare du Nord and of the Place Charles de Gaulle which surrounds the Arc de Triomphe.

It is these objects and the many imperial-looking lamp-standards, all set out like the pieces on a chess-board, that make the Place de la Concorde so beautiful

despite the abominable and ferocious traffic that now surges continually round it. Looking south one sees the classical pediment of the Palais Bourbon or the Assemblée Nationale. This feature, however, bears no relation to the palace which is set at an angle behind it; it was simply tacked on by Napoleon I cheekily hoping to echo the fine, and genuine, frontages of the Crillon and the Hôtel de la Marine opposite the Assemblée on the northern edge of the Place.

The Place de la Concorde from the Hôtel de la Marine

The Place de la Concorde from the south   97

98

The north fountain, River Navigation

The Place de la Concorde: the north fountain

There are two fountains, one either side of the obelisk, in the Place de la Concorde. Identical bronze figures appear round each. I like the silly brazen mermaids, plump and fat-bottomed, dripping with jewellery and clutching their pet fish like plastic bath-toys; they would be more fun than the sober grown-up water spirits sheltering out of the wet behind them. When I drew them they had all been left high and dry while the floodlighting was being seen to and their copper skins were peeling badly after too long in the sun. Beyond them are the magnificent buildings to the north of the square – a glimpse of the Hôtel Crillon on the left, the Hôtel de la Marine on the right, and further away still the cold, correct and stiff pediment of the Madeleine.

In Gabriel's original design for the Place de la Concorde, there was no metal: only stone. The bronze was all added in the reign of Louis-Philippe, along with the obelisk, when Haussmann supervised the refurbishment of the square. The stone was beautifully cleaned up in 1989 for the bicentenary of the French Revolution. But if besides the fountains and the lamps you count the racing traffic and the ranks of parked coaches, most of what you can see in the Place de la Concorde today is metal.

99

The Avenue des Champs-Elysées

The Avenue des Champs-Elysées is not, like Oxford Street or Piccadilly, an enlarged and developed version of a long-established route; indeed, it was not originally there at all. The area was still open fields when in 1667 Le Nôtre, the gardener-designer of the Tuileries, planted lines of trees in parallel rows to extend the gardens' axis westwards; the fields only became Elysian in 1709. Fifteen years later, yet more trees were planted to carry the line on to the summit of the rise, to what is now the Etoile. At its Concorde end the avenue is flanked by greenery, lawns and gardens, echoing the Tuileries foliage but in a more informal way. This is a pleasant place to walk or sit.

Beyond the Rond-Point des Champs-Elysées the greenery is reduced to merely the two lines of trees which stretch away and curve upwards to the Arc de Triomphe, screening from view the glossy and commercial but undistinguished buildings to either side of the avenue. The chestnuts at the left of the picture must stand on dry ground: in the hot summers of 1989 and 1990 they began to turn brown in July, a disconcerting midsummer foretaste of autumn. In spring, in the morning light when the sun is behind you, the Arc de Triomphe looks almost pretty, rising out of a mass of new foliage; but with the light behind it always looks rather forbidding, dispiriting even, with its overtones of war, triumph and death, and with the restless traffic at its feet crawling about like the survivors. It is impossible now to separate this vista from the vision of moving traffic, eight or more abreast. At La Défense the traffic has been banished underground and there is nothing to diminish the contrast between monster buildings and tiny people.

The Marly Horses and the Champs-Elysées

The Grande Arche

The Arc de Triomphe and the Défense Arch

The Arc de Triomphe had two main functions: to look impressive from a distance and to be informative, inspiring and, if possible, beautiful, when seen from close at hand. The bas-reliefs round it are interesting but very uneven. Napoleon commissioned it in 1806 from the architect Chalgrin, but it was thirty years before it was completed. Twelve avenues now radiate from it, and the elegant and uniform if rather brittle buildings which separate them are by Hittorff (of the Place de la Concorde). From the terrace on top of the arch one gets an unforgettable view down all twelve avenues, three or four at a time. Haussmann also got Hittorff to design the Avenue Foch, the widest and the most beautiful of them, which leads to the Bois de Boulogne. Chalgrin's Arch is now surrounded by a deadly whirlpool of traffic and you can only get to it by underground passageway: he would have been astonished and put out at the spectacle.

The Arc de Triomphe

103

Arènes de Lutèce

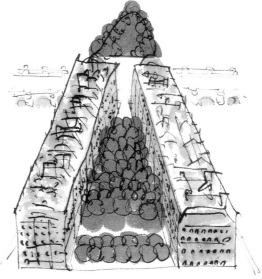

Place Dauphine

Porte St Denis

Bazar de l'Hôtel de Ville

Pyramid, Parc Monceau

Arc de Triomphe

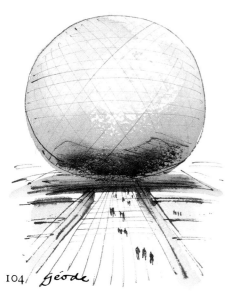

104 Géode

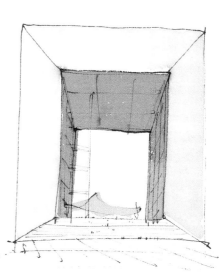

Pyramid

Grande Arche

The Rational City

Buildings are interesting to look at, and to draw, for
different and often contradictory reasons: because they're
very simple, or outrageously heaped with ornamentation;
because they're massive and solid, or thin and spiky; because
they're new and shiny, or old and battered. But even the
most complicated buildings embody or exploit a few basic
elements: repetition, a sense of perspective, economy of
structure, geometrical simplicity. Paris is rich in buildings
that, even if they end up covered with decoration, started
in someone's mind as simple, rational, geometrical shapes.
Lines, squares, triangles and arches, flat and solid, single
or repeated, are what buildings are made of; if they are
repeated often enough they turn into terraces and arcades
and colonnades, or they can be stretched into columns and
towers or extended into long perspectives of stone or grass
or foliage. Rationally conceived and carried out with
imagination, skill and determination, these shapes form
the essential ingredients of elegant, rational Parisian
architecture and city planning.

The simplest form of all, the circle, provided the
ground-plan of the Arènes de Lutèce; given a third dimension,
as a hemisphere, it appears in the many Parisian domes,
originally Jesuitic but more recently nakedly commercial
in purpose; the circle finally reappears in solid form as the
virtually complete sphere of the Géode at La Villette.
Alternatively, the geometric starting point may be a triangle:

Henri IV's Place Dauphine was unusual in being triangular
in plan, and this simple shape is now almost the only
reminder of its original form. The toy stone pyramids in
the Père Lachaise cemetery and in the Parc Monceau, like
the gleaming new transparent one at the Louvre, are really
just sets of triangles made solid. Most buildings of course
are rectangular, though seldom as two-dimensional as that
great archway, the Porte St Denis. Decorative sculptural
incrustations notwithstanding, it really *is* two-dimensional,
no more solid than a rectangular biscuit made in the shape
of an arch. But one could not begin to describe the Arc de
Triomphe adequately in such flat, two-dimensional terms:
it would be meaningless, for seen at an angle, the Arc
de Triomphe is clearly a *solid* object, three arches in one.

The Grande Arche is if anything even more solid. It is
unusual in being a completely new idea – a hollowed-out cube,
a variant on the very idea of an arch so surprising that at
first glance it seems almost unbelievable. All the same, it
seems to have been difficult to find a role for the vast space
created up on top of what are really only two big office
blocks: it all seems astonishing and beautiful, yet also
insubstantial and theatrical. But then of course that's what
triumphal arches are. This one is really just a big square
picture frame or window; a window onto *what*, only time
will tell. What is already certain is that once you've seen
the Grande Arche you can't forget it.

The west side of the Palais Royal

The Palais-Royal

The garden of the Palais-Royal is beautiful and intriguing, because of the mesmeric effect of perspective on simple but almost endlessly repeated architectural units – fluted columns, capitals, arches, windows, balustrades, urns – and also for its effect on the living forms of trees, clipped and trained and regimented into solid, hard-edged shapes. I prefer these long repetitive views to the twin colonnades through which you enter the garden, reminiscent of the colonnades on either side of the Queen's House at Greenwich. Magnificent though these are, they are now marred by their proximity to a sort of petrified forest of short black-and-white decorative stumps, looking both expensive and pointless. But I also like the repetitive elevation of the long building surrounding the garden when seen head on. One sees it best in winter through the bare trees (over the page) when the monotonous alternating pattern of columns and arches creates 500 unbroken metres of stone wallpaper stretching round three sides of the garden.

Alley of pleached limes

The courtyard and the colonnades

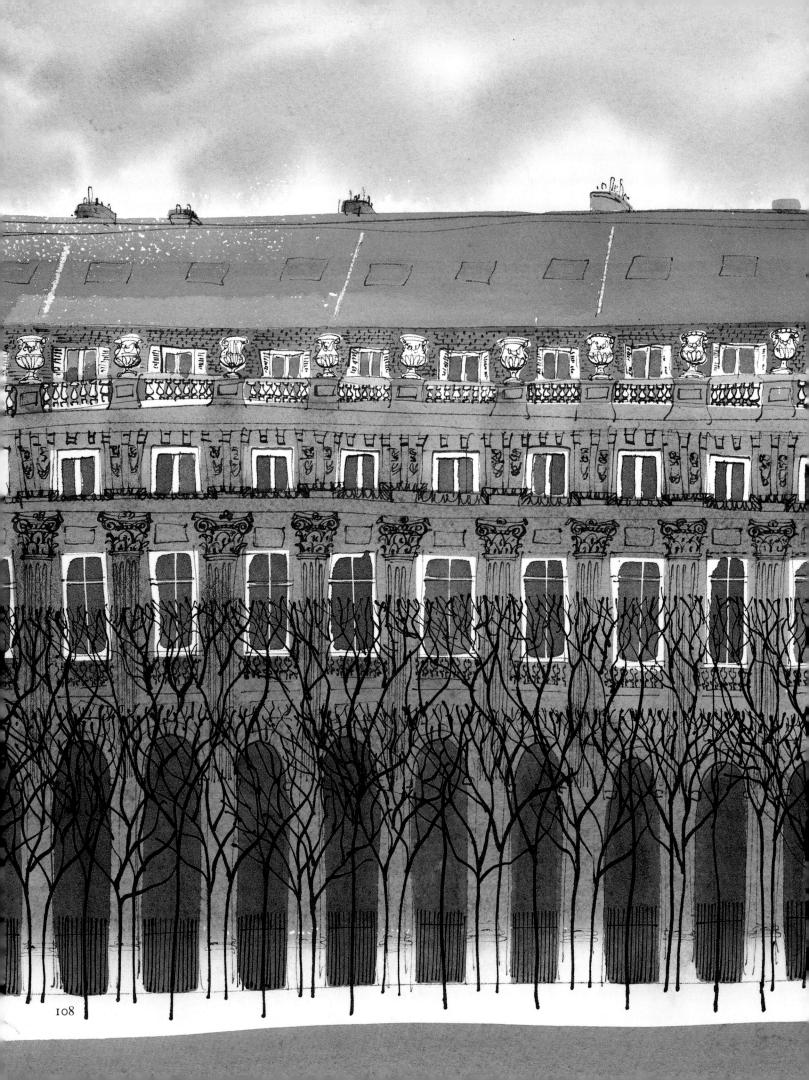

The east side of the Palais Royal

The Rue de Rivoli

No one can look at the Rue de Rivoli and fail to be impressed. It is the city's spinal cord and the most extreme instance of ruthless Parisian determination. To stand at its western extremity with one's back to the Hôtel de la Marine, and to see the perspective of arcades and windows vanish into the distance is a unique Parisian experience.

One curious thing is that its unity is one-sided – it only exists on the north side of the street. To the south are the assorted buildings of the Louvre and the open space of the Tuileries Gardens. In between flows – or stands – the traffic: now a much more conspicuous feature of the street than the souvenir shops, cafés, and money changers beneath its arches. Another odd thing is how casually, needlessly, the unity of the Rue de Rivoli has been broken. Wherever you look along it, but especially from the Tuileries, you see the very destructive way in which individual buildings have been allowed to expand upwards, so that the original modest, beautiful and well-proportioned Mansart roofs have become inflated and top-heavy, and dwarf the original carefully conserved stone elevation that now hangs insignificantly beneath them.

The Rue de Rivoli and the Rue de Castiglione   The Rue de Rivoli

The Domes of Paris

To a Londoner, Paris looks pretty well-off
in the way of domes. Its heights are marked
by domes, the pale grey of the Panthéon
and the white of the Sacré-Cœur; the Jesuits
left a legacy of many elegantly domed
churches; Napoleon left a gilded one with
a sharp point. The one I like best is Libéral
Bruant's dark and austere octagonal dome
over the chapel of the Salpêtrière hospital.

There are other ecclesiastical domes: St
Augustin's, like a fat cactus surrounded by
its pups; or the dumpy top-heavy dome of
Notre-Dame de L'Assomption. But since the
great Jesuit flowering in the seventeenth
century, all the best Parisian domes have
been commercial in purpose, intended to
lend splendour to the new department
stores: there is a very pretty one for Au
Printemps, a self-confident one for the
Bazar de l'Hôtel de Ville, and a real corker
for Félix Potin, the very epitome of strident
enterprise, vulgarity and brashness.

The Salpêtrière

The Panthéon

St Augustin

N-D de l'Assomption

113

Au Printemps

Félix Potin

The Invalides

Parisian perspectives

Not much in Paris has happened by accident. The breathtaking kind of view that suddenly strikes you as you cross a street or round a corner is much more likely to be the result of forethought and endeavour. Sometimes the effect is of classical perfection – of symmetrically receding lines of carefully modelled foliage, or of the mirror-image façades on both sides of the Rue de Castiglione leading up to the Place Vendôme. St Augustin, the Hôtel de Ville, the Madeleine, the Panthéon and the Observatoire are all approached – or at any rate visible – up long and serene avenues of masonry or foliage. Other vistas, though, have appeared complete, in one go, with an almost surrealist exclusion of anything external: the view across or, perhaps, through the Pont de Bir-Hakeim might be a vision of de Chirico's, so completely man-made is it, and so odd in its tension between the Piranesian baroque of the stonework and the spare but strong metal girders that carry the railway.

But there are other views that really *are* happy accidents. There can have been no conscious planning for the way the Rue du Faubourg St Denis and the Rue St

Pont de Bir-Hakeim

Antoine, both pre-Haussmann, curve towards their arches or columns; or for the sudden glimpses that one gets of Notre-Dame through the muddle of the Ile de la Cité; or for the view up the Rue Laffitte towards Notre-Dame de Lorette, perfect enough in its own right, to which at some point was suddenly added the distant new Sacré-Cœur as a kind of unexpected and maybe even unwanted bonus.

Chestnuts in the Avenue de l'Observatoire

Boulevard Malesherbes and St Augustin

Faubourg St Denis

Avenue Victoria

Rue Royale

Quai aux fleurs

Bd Henri IV

Rue Laffitte

Rue St Antoine

115

Parisian public sculpture

Parisian open-air sculpture is assured and accomplished. What's more, it almost always offers a point of view, an instruction or an exhortation – just like a good poster. Notre-Dame's grotesque figures tell us to watch out, mind our step, be good: Morice's statue to the Republic tells us to be loyal, to rally round; Lafayette in the Cours la Reine to be heroic, and Barrias' fine La Défense to be indomitable, to be ready to die and now, by implication, suggests that business too is a battle that has to be waged heroically. Récipon's magnificent quadrigae on the Grand Palais tempt us to cut a dash; but Rodin, in the garden of the Hôtel Biron, says we should reflect first. For even though the Rodin might seem more introspective, more contemplative, it too carries an implicit injuction: to be serious, to try to think things out. Lately, however, such exhortations seem no longer acceptable or even possible. The painted fountains twirling, wiggling and spouting in the Place Igor Stravinsky by the Pompidou Centre seem to carry no message, but to be content to look cheerful and pretty, as if all the important messages have been delivered already and there is nothing left to say. But I think these works do also have clear messages of their own: don't be solemn – have a break – have a giggle – don't worry – be childish. Like pop-songs, they can seem either light-hearted and fun or just plain silly, depending on how one feels.

Place de la République

Notre-Dame

Fountains in the Place Igor Stravinsky

Lafayette, Cours La Reine

Rodin Museum: the Thinker

Quadriga, Grand Palais

La Défense

Bagatelle: The Château

Places, parks and Gardens

Paris doesn't have such numerous and extensive parks as London. It has one enormous park, the Bois de Boulogne, two large and ancient gardens, once royal – the Tuileries and the Luxembourg – and a magnificent herb garden, the Jardin des Plantes; and a number of smaller parks – Buttes Chaumont, Montsouris, Monceau – all created in the mid-nineteenth century by Baron Haussmann. They are all in their different ways beautiful, but with the single exception of the Bois de Boulogne they are much more formal and controlled than English parks; one can tell how carefully they've been laid out, whereas London parks are, or at least try to seem, wilder and more accidental. Now and again a Paris park *does* have a stab at seeming unbuttoned, casual, romantic, in the manner of the Buttes Chaumont. But however charming the effect thus created, *accident* had nothing to do with it: it is obviously very contrived – no more accidental than, say, the design on a piece of willow-pattern pottery.

An earlier and less improbable attempt at informality was the Bagatelle, the pretty enclosed park within the Bois de Boulogne, with its own lakes, grottoes, alleys, pools and fountains. The house itself, seen opposite beyond the lily pond, was built complete with its park in three months by the Count of Artois, later Charles X, in order to win a wager laid with Marie-Antoinette. The Bagatelle is a beautiful place on a spring day, full of bluebells and irises; but it rings with the shrill sound of the park-keepers'

whistles, forbidding picnics and – sin of sins – lying on the grass. Maybe this is a fair price to pay for enjoying green and well-kept lawns in place of bare-trodden earth.

Another delightful Parisian space is the *Square*. This word is evidently not to be understood in any geometrical sense: two of my favourites, the Square du Vert Galant and the Square Barye at the farthest tips of the two islands, are triangular; so are the Square de l'Ile de France and the Square Henri Galli. Most of these *squares* have grass as well as sand, and beautiful trees, and provide much-needed oases of greenery in what is essentially a man-made city. They are all fenced off, carefully maintained, and well provided with seats and benches and litter bins, which remind one, more effectively even than the printed regulations at the gate, that one is here only as a privilege.

The delight of such spaces lies in the contrast between their fairly formal layout and the irrepressible human life they attract. But this is true of most of the city's parks and *places*. This untranslatable word, which covers a variety of public spaces, hints that they all have in common a certain communal significance: places where people can within certain stated conventions relax and enjoy themselves. *Places* in Paris may be as grand as the Place de la Concorde, or little more than an almost imperceptibly widened street, but they all have a certain presence and importance: in them, you know they are not casually chosen stretches of roadway, but special places set aside for people to exist and relax in.

The Parc Montsouris

The Square Marie Curie

The Square Marie Curie

The Parc Montsouris

The Square du Temple

The Square du Temple and the Parc Monceau

Pyramids in the Parc Monceau

The Square du Temple in the northern part of the Marais is a pleasant and recently refurbished patch of greenery, not very big, but with prettily shaded paths and a pond full of ducks. There are many similar small *places*; they all have much in common. They are generally fenced in, and they are all furnished with the same ancient, invariably green-painted ironwork. All are entered through standard metal gates which always bang firmly shut with the same familiar heavy clang. Their voluminous regulations are set out on a standard and indestructible cast-iron notice board; drinking fountains,

wire rubbish-baskets and wooden benches also are standard. Bigger *places*, like parks, have chalet-like huts – most now sadly the worse for wear – for their guardians, and identical rustic bridges of concrete appear wherever there is a stream to cross. Such standardisation might sound monotonous, but the items are good and serviceable and in general it works well: one doesn't really mind having seen all the ingredients before.

The warm summer evening in the Parc Monceau reminded me vividly of the Lodi Gardens in New Delhi: lightly-clad seated figures enjoying the air among foliage and

semi-exotic architecture. As well as fine trees, there are a number of picturesque ruins in the park, mostly conventionally classical – columns, colonnades, tombs, and a rocky hillock, all of them the remnants of an intensive effort at beautification by Philippe Egalité, the Duc de Chartres. There are also two small pyramids, only slightly ruined, which I particularly like. The park was laid out in 1778; its gardener was a Scotsman. It's not very big, but its paths are ingeniously arranged and screened so that one can walk it from end to end four times and hardly recross one's steps.

Place Dr Antoine Béclère

The Place Dr Antoine Béclère and the Parc des Buttes Chaumont

Paris is supplied with a profusion of minor resting-places. There are many good solid benches under the trees in the streets as well as in the parks, where one can pause and enjoy the surrounding scene for a minute or two without having to make a special journey. And there are places where a street widens out, as when it is about to divide in two, that allow enough space for a small garden or square. One such is the Place Dr Antoine Béclère in the Rue du Faubourg St Antoine, beyond the Bastille: hardly more than a shaded patch of ground between the two lines of traffic, yet a peaceful haven in a busy working street. On the Saturday afternoon when I was there

it was peopled mainly by men, pausing on the way home with the afternoon's shopping to read the paper or play *boules*. The Faubourg St Antoine would be a duller and more businesslike place without this pleasant green oasis. On the other hand, you would hardly choose it as a place to spend a whole afternoon off. You'd go instead to the Luxembourg Gardens, or the Tuileries, or to the most picturesque-looking park of them all, the Buttes Chaumont. This has for its fine centre-piece a precipitous mountain, tree-clad and vaguely Chinese in style but topped by a small Greek temple. The path up it is fenced in by the same unlifelike yet endearing concrete branches as appear in

the other parks. It all looks too good to be true, and so of course it is, being made up partly of real, partly of artificial, rocks. Massed parties of schoolchildren now run organised races round it. The whole thing was dreamed up in an uncharacteristically romantic moment by the indefatigable Haussmann, on what had previously been a grisly area of old chalk workings, rubbish dumps and horse-bones. But the Buttes Chaumont park offers an unforgettably beautiful vision all the same – a vision pounced on by the many Japanese who get married in the nearby Mairie of the district and then spill out onto the Buttes Chaumont grass to have their wedding pictures taken.

Parc des Buttes Chaumont

A crossroads at Père Lachaise

The Père Lachaise Cemetery

Cemeteries in the past had the same planning advantage as golf courses have now, in securing green areas within urban developments. If you stand on a vantage point in central Paris – on the roof terrace of the Arab Institute, for example – and look east, you see in the distance a large patch of greenery among the grey roofs. The trees are those of the Père Lachaise cemetery, and they give the area a surprisingly verdant air. Père Lachaise stands on rising ground on the site of a Jesuit house of retreat; it became a cemetery in 1802. On a fine day it offers a pleasant couple of hours' wandering in the shade. The place is peopled by strollers, map in hand and sometimes of sinister aspect, and by an army of gardeners and other tidiers-up.

Père Lachaise is an unlikely jumble of unrelated architectural bric-à-brac, its pyramids and stupas, basalt bathing-huts and marble dog-kennels oddly assorted but marshalled with military precision into tidily numbered divisions. These are separated by long, straight wooded avenues and winding lanes, some incongruously marked 'One way' or 'No entry', as if for traffic. It was ingeniously laid out by Brongniart, the architect of the Paris

Bourse; and, because of its oddly assorted architectural bedfellows, it is fascinating in a surrealist sort of way. Egyptian, classical, Gothic, Indian and other styles fight for one's attention, in sizes ranging from modest to mega-stupendous. Many famous people have been buried here; sentiment or some vague curiosity may impel one to seek out a special tomb. But although some of them are pretty, or strange, or funny, I cannot help finding Père Lachaise in the end a pathetic and dispiriting place. There are more appropriate, more vivid ways of remembering Colette or Cherubini or Corot than by gazing at these bits of stone. The very notion of leaving a physical monument behind one now seems silly, and all this long-term commemoration merely a self-important and ludicrous form of pollution.

The cemetery also has more genuine but grimmer associations: it was here that the Communards in 1871 made their final desperate stand. The last 147 of them were shot at dawn on 28 May against a wall, the Mur des Fédérés, in the south-west corner of the cemetery. Its tombs must have provided almost impenetrable cover for insurgents; it's surprising that Haussmann hadn't had the lot cleared away.

Avenue Transversale No 2

Père Lachaise classical, Gothic and Egyptian motifs

April in the Bois de Boulogne

The Bois de Boulogne

Even in early April, when everything is fresh
and beautiful, parts of the Bois de Boulogne
are on a weekday almost deserted – trees
stretch away on every side and one can even
feel momentarily lost, as if in a forest in a
fairy-story. But though at this time of year,
the leaves are out the undergrowth isn't
yet, so one can see quite a long way; and
one is soon brought back to the present by
the sight of a distant horseman or car. Such
activity as there may be is not very energetic:
groups of anglers appear at the edge of the
lake and men play *boules* along the sandy
rides. But later on, as the season advances
and the foliage thickens, the place fills up.
By the beginning of May, and especially on
the May Day holiday, it is bursting with life:
walkers, joggers, couples and families, the
solitary and the gregarious, mostly armed
with bottles of water and all determined to
make the most of the day and the season.

The Bois was a wild and dangerous place
until the 1850s, when Alphand laid it out
– supposedly on the lines of Hyde Park,
though the similarity is hard to detect now.
Perhaps this is because many of the biggest
trees were cut down for firewood during
the Commune. But it hasn't been entirely
tamed, and even now it's thought best to
avoid it at dusk and at night.

Fishing and Boules in the Bois

May Day by the Lac Inférieur

The Musée d'Orsay

Visitors' Paris

There are a few places in Paris that no visitor can afford to miss. Sooner or later, whether one really wants to or not, everyone goes to the Louvre, the Pompidou Centre, the Musée d'Orsay, the Eiffel Tower and Montmartre: they are so famous that you just couldn't admit you'd been to Paris and not seen them. They are all fascinating experiences, though their fame means they are often quite hard to get into; the queues at the Louvre and at the Musée d'Orsay are spectacles in themselves and they give one a sense of achievement at merely reaching the ticket office.

Now and again there is in a museum a close rapport between building and exhibits: in the Musée Carnavalet in the Marais, for example, Parisian history – and especially Revolutionary history – is enshrined and explained in a mansion that is itself part of that history; just as, in the Musée Cluny, medieval sculpture and tapestries can be seen in a medieval building. But in the Louvre, the contrast is between the vitality of the milling crowds and the impassive treasures they have come to see. And the interest of the Hôtel Salé, now the Picasso Museum, lies in the vivid contrast between the sumptuousness of the setting – its graceful Renaissance decoration, whose very essence consists in art constrained by ancient conventions – and the mould-breaking individuality, itself so revolutionary, of the Picasso works it now houses.

At the Centre Pompidou too the contrasts, tensions even, are strong: between works of art which were originally rebellious and disruptive, and a reverent setting in which they are pinned down into a scholarly sequence like mounted butterflies. At the Pompidou irrepressible humanity is kept safely outside in the big square, in a scene of unforgettable vitality, mischief and of squalor.

Many famous Parisian sights are of military origin. Where martial glorification is concerned, I like the seventeenth-century monuments better than those from Napoleonic and later times. I much prefer the splendid Invalides exterior and its great inner courtyard, where war is formalised into a conventional matter of helmets and breastplates, to Napoleon's tomb with its soupy aura of nineteenth-century idolatry and propaganda. That century is better represented in Paris by its practical ingenuity – Métro, boulevards, the Eiffel Tower – than by its romantic obsession with *la Gloire*.

Twenty million visitors a year is a lot for any city to absorb, and it's not surprising that the more fragile of the Parisian honey-pots have cracked. In Montmartre, it is the place itself that has been turned into a museum, or rather a theme park; a caricature of the idea of Bohemian artistic life, of wild piratical portraitists and eager victims, with the Place du Tertre at its rackety rip-off core. But parts of Montmartre had of course long ago been made famous by Utrillo and photographers like Atget and Brassaï – it was Brassaï who took the definitive picture of one of the beautiful flights of steps that lead up to the Sacré-Cœur. Such sights can withstand a good deal of fame and exposure without being harmed. And even now one doesn't have to walk very far from the commercialism of the Place du Tertre to find that the crowds have thinned away and the peeling walls, the pavements and the domed vistas seem almost unchanged over the years.

Picasso and the Musée Carnavalet

The surprising and delightful thing about this beautiful museum devoted to Picasso, is how well the artist's works accord with their sumptuous Renaissance setting. In these extremely grand rooms, the skills and intelligence of each enhance the other: the conventional and perfected craftsmanship of the seventeenth century setting off the bright, sharp, yet sensuous wit and invention of the twentieth. Everything about the fabric of the Hôtel Salé would be memorable even without the Picassos. The grand gateway and the cobbled courtyard, the fine staircase inside, the sculptured figures over the doorways, and the views of the nearby Marais houses give one a clear impression of the grandeur and the environment of this old Parisian house.

The Musée Picasso

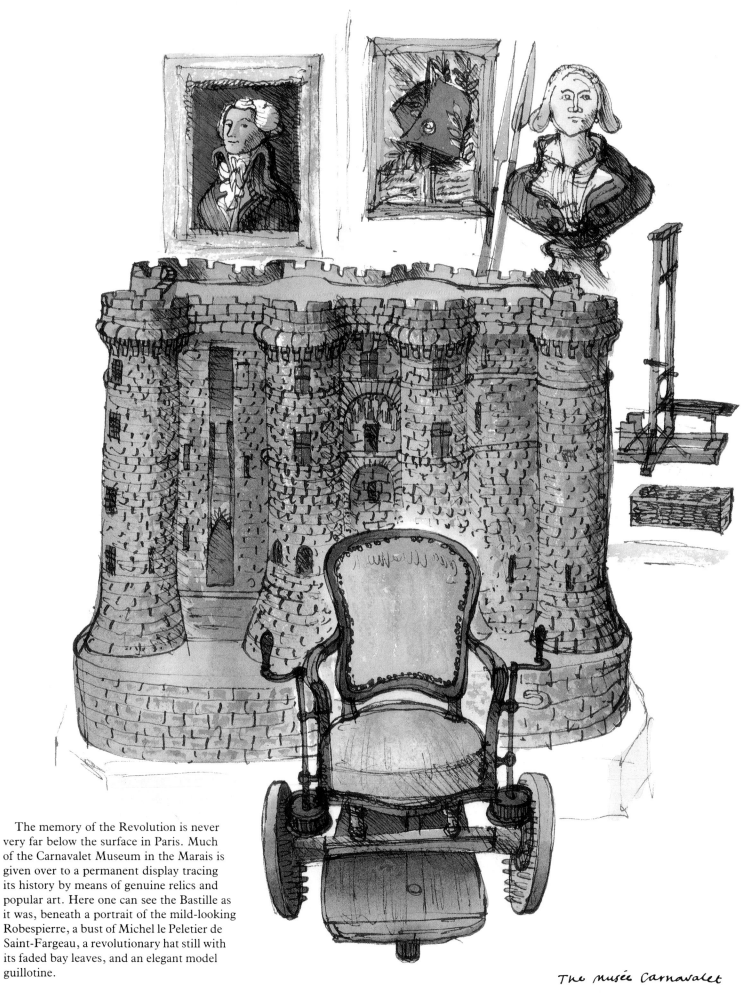

The memory of the Revolution is never very far below the surface in Paris. Much of the Carnavalet Museum in the Marais is given over to a permanent display tracing its history by means of genuine relics and popular art. Here one can see the Bastille as it was, beneath a portrait of the mild-looking Robespierre, a bust of Michel le Peletier de Saint-Fargeau, a revolutionary hat still with its faded bay leaves, and an elegant model guillotine.

The Musée Carnavalet

The Centre Georges Pompidou

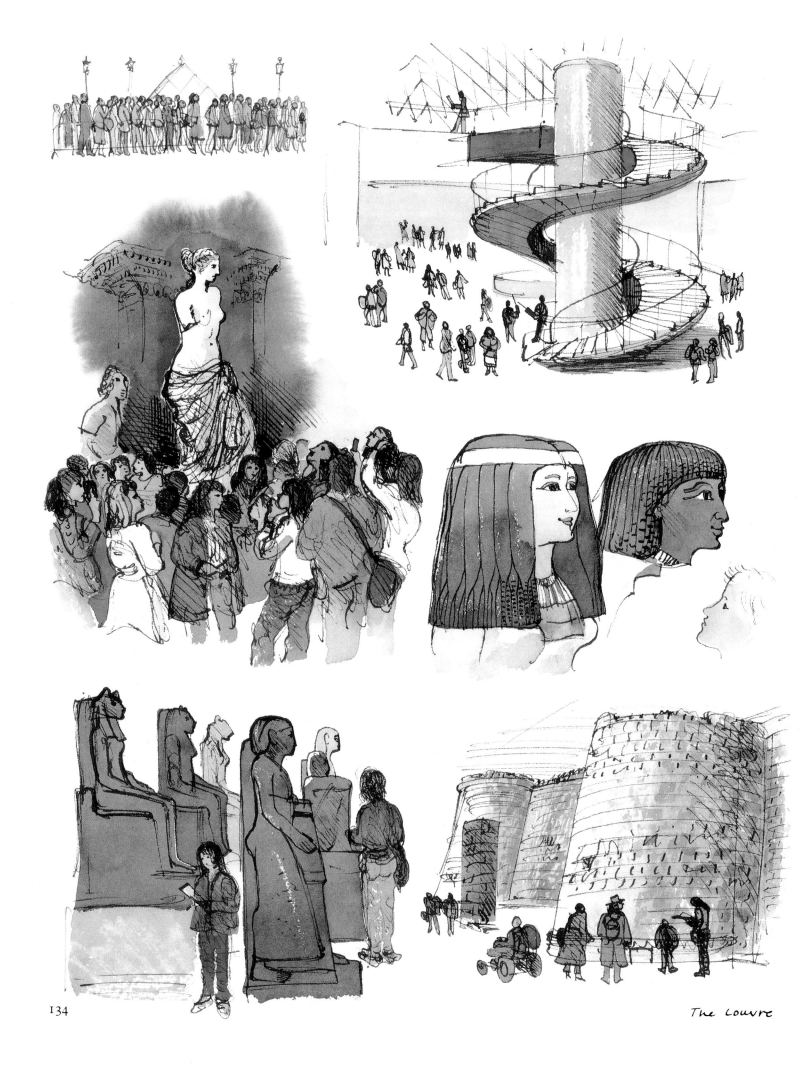

The Louvre

The Musée du Louvre

The Louvre is part palace, part museum, part endurance test: a perplexing mixture of conflicting experiences. I find it hard to concentrate on the exhibits because the other visitors are so interesting; coming, of course, from as many different places and cultures as the things they've all come to see. In the end one has to enjoy both aspects of the experience – the sculptures and artefacts on the one hand, the milling and eager people on the other.

I suppose that, imagining beforehand a visit to a great museum, one thinks it will offer one-to-one confrontations with works of art, as if looking at reproductions in a catalogue. But of course it is a much richer experience: in two ways. To begin with, photographs can't give one any real idea of the movement and swirl of the *Winged Victory*, of the way in which every least touch of the sculptor's hand is intent on suggesting both solid shape and springing movement, so that one can almost feel the air which presses and tugs the drapery against the flesh. I'd never properly noticed this until I tried to draw it: it's odd how powerfully the impression can still survive after so many centuries.

Secondly, the *Winged Victory* wasn't originally meant to be an isolated treasure, an ikon, a masterpiece: it was just a job to be done well and a thing to be seen. The people looking up at it from the great staircase in the Louvre, appraising, awestruck, mystified, fed-up or simply worn-out, made me feel that it's better to see a work of art being responded to, however distractingly, than to study it in sanctified but sterile isolation.

The Winged Victory

The Invalides

Handsome ramparts topped by batteries of historic cannon surround the Jardin des Invalides. Once inside the great arched doorway, the Cour d'Honneur is a spectacle of considerable majesty: a great square stone courtyard, the perspectives and the patterning of whose stone setts are fascinating in themselves. It is surrounded on all four sides by an arcaded ground floor and a nobly proportioned upper storey with handsome ornamental surrounds to the veterans' attic windows. Standing about under the arches are some more old cannon and a few fragments of heroic sculpture, including the shattered and legless torso of a martial figure – a little tactless, one might think, in this context.

No particular irony, however, seems to be attached to the two relics in the far left corner of the courtyard. The primitive Renault tank of 1916, like an ugly beetle in its heavy bolted-together crudity and brutishness, is nearer to the very earliest railway locomotives than to this century's mechanised weaponry. The peaceful-looking old Paris taxi, also built by Renault, was one of the thousands pressed desperately into service to carry the French army to the Marne in 1914, much as armies today fly to minor war zones in incongruously jolly-looking commercial jets.

Napoleon's Tomb is not really my cup of tea. Napoleon had been dead in St Helena for nineteen years when in 1840 his body was dug up and shipped back to France for its funeral. Twenty-one years later still,

Les Invalides: the Cour d'Honneur

The first Renault tank

One of the Marne taxis

having lain meanwhile in one of the chapels in the Eglise du Dôme, it was finally installed in this large subterranean tomb. You can look down onto it through a circular hole in the floor of the church, but to inspect it properly you must descend into the crypt, as if into a particularly opulent Turkish bath or an indoor swimming-pool of majestic proportions. The tomb, of polished porphyry the colour of dried blood, stands on the green granite floor of the pool. It is surrounded by twelve improbably big angels standing with folded wings and holding wreaths and other symbolic props. Their scale seems an error of judgement on the part of the architect Visconti – if real people get too close to colossal stone figures, the latter look silly. It was a relief to climb back up to dry land.

The ramparts of the Jardin des Invalides

Napoleon's tomb in the Eglise du Dôme

Montmartre: The Sacré-Coeur

Montmartre

One can't go far in Paris without glimpsing, far away on the northern skyline, the white domes of the Sacré-Cœur. The church stands on a hilltop with a magnificent view across the city. For a closer look, one has to climb one of several long flights of steps – choosing either the central monumental route, open to the sky, or minor but prettier stairways that climb up between houses and trees, with pretty lamp-standards and well-made railings to cling to, and level places to recover your breath after each short flight of steps.

To the west of it is Montmartre proper. This, too, is a tourist Mecca, centred on the rackety Place du Tertre, a once beautiful small square now given over to a sort of commercialised parody of the Bohemian artists' life, and filled in summer with bemused spectators being sketched and mercilessly chatted-up. But only a few steps away are pleasant and quieter streets (see pages 140–141) which remind one of what a pretty and genuinely picturesque quarter this once was, a place where real painters could get on with their job in peace.

The Rue Maurice Utrillo

139

GALERIE

AUBERGE DE LA B

ANCIENNEMENT
des BILLARS EN BOIS

AUBERGE DE LA BONNE FRANQUETTE

CAFE

The Rue St Rustique

The Place Blanche and the
Boulevard Poissonnière

At night the Place Blanche and the wide Boulevard de Clichy are stuffed with parked coaches with their engines running. The air is heady with their fumes and the people have a determined if bemused desire for entertainment. But in the daytime the shaded central lane of the Boulevard is quieter and more homely, with families relaxing on the benches and people heading for the Métro with their heavy shopping – not at all the raffish Gay Paree that one half expected to find there. Like Guimard's Métro entrances, Morris columns are an evocative feature of the busier Parisian pavements, their posters for plays and circuses and exhibitions enhancing the impression of a lively and adventurous city – often with good, bold, startling images. Some Morris columns are very grand, glazed and rotating; others are simple and cardboardy, like fireworks.

The Place Blanche and the Moulin Rouge

Parisian cinema posters tend to be duller than those for plays – more reliant on photographs and much more predictable. There are plenty of different ones along the front of the Cinéma Rex on the Boulevard Poissonnière, a big building comprising seven smaller cinemas and 2800 seats. Here it is the ebullient architecture rather than the graphics that has style and vitality. It was built in 1932, and despite the blank walls appropriate to cinemas it looks lively and fun; it is topped by a concrete wedding cake. Monster cinemas are an important element on the Parisian boulevards – almost as much a part of the scene as the planes and acacias and the cheerful café tables, and the very ordinary pavement activities that go hurrying on heedless of the dream world of the posters up above them.

The Cinéma Rex on the Boulevard Poissonnière

The Vendôme Column and the Eiffel Tower

The Place Vendôme would appear to be the
most perfectly unified concept imaginable
– a handsome rectangular ground plan
with the corners trimmed off to turn it into
an octagon; fine houses all round it, all built
to an identical pattern; entered by two roads
only, one at each end, so that it is free of
cross-traffic; the whole designed as a perfect
setting for the magnificent bronze column
at its centre. But although the fronts of the
buildings appear indeed just as they were
conceived (in about 1685, by the architect
Hardouin-Mansart), the houses behind them
were only completed as buyers appeared,
many of them only after Hardouin-
Mansart's death – a notable confirmation
of his original vision. The column itself
appeared a century later, in 1806–10,
replacing an equestrian statue of Louis
XIV – a much more modest centre-piece
perhaps, but certainly one more in key
with the seventeenth-century splendour
of the whole *place*. The bronze for the
column was obtained by melting down
250 Austrian and Russian cannon taken
at Austerlitz. In 1870, it was felled to the
ground by Communards led by the painter
Courbet. None of this could be guessed at
from the square's present serene,
impregnable and expensive air. The
imperial figure at the top is Napoleon, though

144

The Place Vendôme and the Ritz

even he was deposed at the Restoration to be replaced for a while by an innocuous fleur-de-lys.

The Eiffel Tower, by contrast, owed little to its existing surroundings. Although it stands on the same axis as the Ecole Militaire, and although the walk up the Parc du Champ de Mars provides the best approach to it, the Ecole Militaire is too far away to play more than a token rôle. From close to, the Eiffel Tower becomes instead a monster arch, a gigantic and confusing agglomeration of brown latticed girders, tiny staircases, red and yellow lifts, and queues. It's from further away that it really grabs you; glimpsed unexpectedly from almost anywhere in the city, it is an appropriate and unforgettable symbol of nineteenth-century ingenuity, determination and courage, commemorating only the determination of its remarkable creator.

The Champ de Mars and the Eiffel Tower

The Métro Barbès Rochechouart

The Working City

In Montmartre or at the Louvre, on the Pont des Arts or in front of the Pompidou Centre, it's easy to forget that Paris has any other function than to attend to the needs and the whims of visitors. But one only has to step off the boulevard or into the Métro to remember that this is also a much more surprising city, one intent on earning its living and preoccupied with things that visitors don't usually notice or bother about: commuting, getting down to work in businesses and offices, buying and selling things that are only incidentally aimed at the visitor. These are *real* activities, interesting to observe and not hard to find. If for example one takes the Métro from Châtelet to Anvers, the stop for Montmartre, one has to change at Barbès Rochechouart, climbing in the process from underground to mid-air, past the curious and essentially Parisian scene opposite. Then again, if one stops to have a look at the much grander railway termini, their architecture offers some curious insights into the French attitude to rail travel, at times stately, at others frivolous. So too with the office buildings: there is a startling contrast between the showy and commercial nineteenth-century splendour of the various central banks and the spare utilitarian elegance of a great working building like the newspaper office of *Le Parisien* in the Rue Réaumur.

In the smartest parts of the city, although work is going on all around you, it's often hidden away behind plate glass and one's attention is distracted by other things. Out on the Grands Boulevards though, *work* is inescapable – the pavements thronged by people getting to or from it or pushing it about in the form of newly-made dresses or wheelbarrows full of bread. The pavements are the scene of plentiful commerce in goods and services – anything from plastifying your documents to roasting you a chicken or selling you a balloon. Paris would be a duller place if all these activities were to move upmarket and indoors.

Even the humdrum down-to-earth business of keeping the city clean and tidy turns out to be an expert, dramatic and highly co-ordinated affair. So too is the task of keeping Parisian foliage green and orderly and properly at bay – an operation which may now and then suffer a dramatic reverse.

I enjoy looking at these scenes and activities and drawing them, because they are surprising: less attention is usually paid to them than to the accepted sights of Paris. They are also very good to draw: people at work make interesting, intent subjects, though you have to keep out of their way. In the course of working on this book, I came to think that trying to draw someone sweeping the street or launching a wind-up plastic pigeon is not only harder but more interesting than drawing a building that stands there stock-still until you get tired of looking at it.

The Métro

The Paris Métro is one of the city's most durable assets. The old bits have worn well, the new are models of their kind. The system was extremely well thought out in the first place. The large, elliptically arched tunnels are wide enough for both tracks and the stations are big, airy and without claustrophobia. It is fairly quiet: most of the trains run on pneumatic rubber tyres, not with a thundery roar but with a gentle swish. The carriages are upright and traditional-looking, box-shaped and rectangular in section; they don't look as if they've had to be distorted to fit into a round tunnel, as in London. The latest rolling stock, to be seen on Line One, is as sure-footed an example of industrial design as are the RER coaches, by the designer Roger Tallon. You can stand upright in the coaches, even at the sides; there is no interior glass, and you have an unbroken view of the whole carriage. You open the doors yourself; the door handles are firm and solid; when they are about to close,

Bir-Hakeim

automatically, a hooter sounds. If you are interested in the track, you can look through the window behind the driver's back, observe the gradients and the sharp curves, and understand, for example, why the tyres screech on the tight bend just

outside the Bastille station. The Métro runs on various unpredictable levels: a train can be high over the river one moment and yet be on the lower track at the next station.

The cast-iron art-nouveau station entrances by Guimard have long been recognised as

The Porte de St Cloud platform at Mabillon, Line Ten

Underground concourse at Châtelet - Les Halles

classics; the older platforms are less famous,
but none the less beautiful with their bold
blue-and-white tiled station names and
their long wooden benches. Many of these
still remain, especially on Line Ten from
Boulogne to Austerlitz. So on the whole
do the traditional Métro surfaces: white
glazed tiles, carefully laid with only the
narrowest infilling of mortar in between.
Recently relaid tiles, as in the new London
tube stations, are more carelessly and
coarsely laid, with lots of mortar to make
the job easier, quicker and cheaper.

The long corridors at many Métro
stations offer pitches for people to sell
flowers, fluorescent sweets, leather goods
and fruit; and for musicians. These last
also ride the trains, filling a carriage with
music or din for a station or two before
passing the hat and disappearing. Most
are not up to the standard of pavement
performers: only a captive audience would
put up with them. People also beg
unashamedly in the carriages, and a few
people use the platform as their daytime
homes – bedding down on the benches,
plastic bags full of their food and possessions
beside them, their pee trickling across the
platform towards the tracks.

Rush hour on Line Two

Mid-morning on Line One

The Gare du Nord

The great Parisian railway stations

From in front, the Parisian railway termini look calm and grand. They do not vie with each other to tempt one to use a particular line, but their majesty dignifies, even glorifies, the notion of getting from one place to another. Behind the imposing façades, the stations look much more of a muddle as their once beautiful and logical nineteenth-century structures undergo the desperate adaptations and changes of mind of later engineers or Museum directors.

The Gare de l'Est has a long and decorative frontage. But the grandest and most splendid Parisian terminus is the Gare du Nord by the architect Hittorff, who also worked on the Place de la Concorde and the Place de l'Etoile. Hittorff did nothing by halves: to avoid uncertainty, he repeated NORD eight times. He also embellished the station's skyline with nine

forbidding female figures, each crowned with a small castle and meant to represent the spirit of one of the cities served by the line. It's hard to imagine such an idea crossing the channel – King's Cross, say, weighed down by Miss Yorks and Miss Newcastles. Hittorff stuck eight equally proud regional figures, complete with identical castellated crowns but this time seated, on the stone pavilions in the Place de la Concorde. Other figures not dissimilar in spirit sit on the parapet of the old Gare d'Orsay looking down on the chilly Seine – the one in the drawing opposite represents Poitiers, one of a trio now looked after by the Musée d'Orsay as carefully as the bronze animals on its forecourt. Some years ago, when the station had already closed down but its beautiful hotel was still extant, I stayed there in a fine

bedroom whose bath, enormous and gushing, had golden claw feet and whose oval *œil-de-bœuf* window looked out over the roof-tops to the Eiffel Tower and the sunset.

These northern station goddesses are all dignified, severe of mien, warmly and sensibly if classically dressed, and all look as impregnable as their castellated crowns. But on the surface of the Gare de Lyon, serving the warm and hedonistic Midi, float sexier and more lightly-clad figures, suggesting not civic virtues but southern vitality and availability. Behind them, looking down on the platforms, is the Train Bleu restaurant, a sort of VIP lounge and a splendid monument to warmth, wealth, vigour and all the liberating magic of the French Riviera.

The Gare de Lyon

The old Gare d'Orsay

DÉPART GRANDES LIGNES
BILLETS - Information - Reservations

The Gare de l'Est

The Crédit Lyonnais on the
Boulevard Montmartre

The Banque Nationale de Paris
in the Rue de l'Echiquier

152

Banks and business buildings

Paris has some very splendid banks – artistic but solid, and covered with cascades of symbolic but respectable statuary to allay depositors' anxieties, their mighty roofs echoing those of the grandest château or Hôtel de Ville. The finest are in or near the Boulevards des Italiens, Haussmann, and Montmartre, just north of the Bourse. This last is a much less flamboyant building than the banks, surrounded by a forest of sober classical columns, its approaches marked by Métro entrances, allegorical sculptures, news-stands and public lavatories.

To the east of the Bourse runs the long, straight Rue Réaumur, sparkling with more lavishly adorned commercial buildings, some of them forced into strangely contorted shapes by the awkward and angular building sites left where a rigid new Haussmann boulevard overlaid and clashed with the old street plan. Such bizarre effects can be seen at their most extreme just south-west of the Porte St Denis. But among the Rue Réaumur offices stands another kind of building altogether. It has a spare and austere façade of painted steel; its decoration is restrained and almost inseparable from its structure, its surface patterning consisting solely of the bolts that hold it together. This office, orginally designed for the newspaper *Le Parisien* by the architect G. Chédanne in 1904–5, is as startlingly modern as Guimard's Métro entrances. It looks remarkable even now, because it clearly stood at the turning-point when lavishly applied decoration, however beautiful, must suddenly have begun to look like icing, or camouflage.

The reason for the high quality of the Rue Réaumur's office buildings is simple but ingenious. The city offered six gold medals every year for the best new building and the winning owners' property taxes were cut by half. A walk eastwards along the street as far as the Boulevard de Sébastopol confirms the competitions' success. This Sentier district is interesting anyway, for its mixture of wealthy and long-established businesses and exotic curiosities like the shopping arcades or passages that burrow unpredictably between the streets. Some of these passages have prospered; others are intriguingly shabby, full of tropical fruit and vegetables, wigs, toupees and false moustaches. Even the offices, while splendidly enriched with good lettering and well-carved decoration, clearly belong to the vanished era before computers and fork-lift trucks, an era when heavy goods were trundled into the office's courtyard on a miniature railway. Only the track and the turntable junction are left now as tantalising reminders.

*office of Le Parisien,
124 Rue Réaumur*

Pavement tradespeople

You could live perfectly well in Paris without ever having to set foot inside a shop: everything you need, from basic essentials like bread and fish and vegetables to cooked chickens and wind-up plastic pigeons, live lobsters and balloons as big as people, can be bought on the pavement. Some of these things come from stalls that are simply outdoor extensions of shops. Many restaurants, even quite expensive ones, keep their crabs, oysters, crayfish and other shellfish outside in the fresh air on pretty stalls whose shelves are decorated with ice, seaweed and lemons. Other salespeople are more or less mobile, depending on whether their stalls are on wheels or castors. Some of these movable stalls have a home-made look, some are lavish and electric; all have to be pushed home, or inside, at night. But the commonest and simplest of these enterprises is carried on out of a suitcase or a large shoulder bag, by the Algerian and Moroccan hawkers who operate wherever enough people, especially visitors, are passing – conspicuously in the Place de la Concorde or in front of the Sacré-Cœur, or more obscurely in the passages of the Métro. These salesmen, though tough and strong, often look at the end of their tether – it must be a ground-down, interminable and unrewarding way to earn a living, and it suggests that the French haven't managed to absorb their ex-colonial citizens as well as used to be claimed.

Of course, on the pavements as elsewhere, the trend is towards uniformity – the same monster fibreglass oranges, half-open to dispense freshly-squeezed juice and to provide a showcase for people looking for work, can be seen in many different places all over the city; many of the pavement oyster stalls belong to one single booming chain of restaurants. So it's good to see the home-made, the makeshift and the individual surviving in the shape of cardboard flower boxes made into temporary counters, and flotillas of home-made yachts being steered home on four old bicycle wheels. And I enjoy seeing the morning's new bread being delivered by the armful on foot, or being pushed along the pavement in a small wheeled pram-like basket, instead of starting its brief but essential existence in the back of a van.

Faubourg St Denis   Quai du Louvre   Faubourg St Denis

Rue Vieille du Temple   Pont des Arts   Pont des Arts

Faubourg St Denis   Pont Au Change   Bonne Nouvelle

Pont au Double   Place du Parvis du Sacré-Cœur

Faubourg St Denis   Boulevard Ornano   Pont des Arts   Rue de Dunkerque

Boulevard St Denis   Porte Dauphine   Jardin des Tuileries

Boulevard Montmartre   Boul' Mich   Rue du Faubourg St Denis   Boulevard de Magenta

Boulevard St Germain   Rue Berger   Rue St Jacques   Square Willette   Quai du Louvre

155

Parisian shopping

I look now at the shop-windows in the Rue
St Honoré in much the same way as I used
as a student to look at the tantalisingly laid
tables of Parisian restaurants; and, as then,
walk on. The famous names along this
star-studded street are renowned and
mouthwatering; different from the
restaurants in that they are not just shops
but the flagships of far-flung commercial
empires.

The Place de la Madeleine offers shoppers
and non-shoppers from the Rue St Honoré
a refuge and a leisurely cup of tea. All the
same, it's difficult to warm to the Madeleine
itself: it's too much like the Paris Bourse with
a pediment added, or a second National
Assembly. For some reason the same
problem does not arise with classical
buildings in London, where they fit more
easily into the whole street. But in the Place
de la Madeleine it's as if the Parthenon itself
had been plonked down among the
Peugeots and the pigeons.

Parisian shopping arcades, and shop-
fronts too, can be of extreme discretion
and elegance, or the reverse. Biberon,
in the Rue St Honoré, is prepared to let you
know who it is in an unemphatic sort of way,
but I couldn't find the radio shop's name
anywhere – unless it was called Promotion.
The shops that I shall miss are the corner
bread shops and *pâtisseries*, elegant and
very pretty but not overdone. It will be a
pity when they've all been turned into
boutiques.

The Place de la Madeleine

Rue St Honoré

Galerie St Marc

Passage des Panoramas

Passage Brady

334 Rue St Honoré

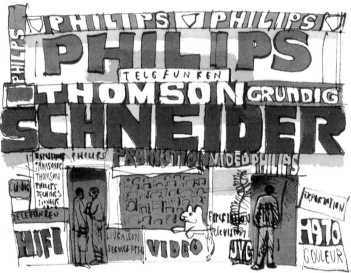

Boulevard de Sébastopol

Rue du Château

Rue des Francs-Bourgeois

Rue Raymond Losserand

157

saturday shopping in the Faubourg St Antoine

The Faubourg St Antoine and the Faubourg St Denis

I particularly like two shopping streets that extend beyond the old city boundaries into what was at one time the Faubourg or suburb. One is the Rue du Faubourg St Antoine, which begins at the Bastille and runs eastward through the furniture-making district. There are still plenty of signs of this activity in the alleys and courtyards running off the main street, but I really like the street for other reasons: in particular for its vigorous if slightly down-at-heel style – cheap but lively, and without pretensions. It is a working-class area and there are many north Africans here; there are Tunisian and Moroccan signs on the shop fronts and higher up the walls. It's a busy place on a Saturday afternoon, serving the mixed, sometimes exotic needs of a partly immigrant community along with the universal commodities of bread, meat, cheese, vegetables, and wine. Here more importance attaches to these basic needs than to other things some might think desirable, like newer cars or newer clothes. Eventually, the Rue du Faubourg St Antoine widens and then splits at the pretty Place Dr Antoine Béclère (page 122).

Something of the same flavour attaches to the Rue du Faubourg St Denis, which can be seen in the drawing curving away to the right beyond the archway. It too is full of butchers and greengrocers and kebab stalls and shops selling wigs. It is the extension northwards of the Rue St Denis which is patrolled by numerous splendidly-attired prostitutes. The Rue du Faubourg St Denis is soberer and more mundane, but fascinating all the same.

Rue St Denis

The Porte St Denis

If one has seen later triumphal arches, the Porte St Denis of 1672 looks large and impressive but extremely thin front-to-back – like a big hoarding erected to advertise something. This is just what it is – a celebration of Louis XIV's victories on the Rhine. It was obviously meant to be looked *through*, not seen end-on. The arrival of the Grands Boulevards must have created a problem here, for now as you approach the Porte St Denis crosswise along the Boulevard de Bonne Nouvelle all you see at first is a sort of tall, thin faceless wafer of stone. But the proper frontal view of the archway, seeming to dwarf the tall houses around it, makes a fine piece of theatre.

159

Trees, pavements and parking

Though Paris is rather meagrely supplied with open green spaces, there are plenty of fine trees along the avenues and on the boulevards, and often in the smaller streets too. They are a key element in those boulevards where the Métro runs overhead, where lines of plane trees run alongside the raised girders and soften their grey and mechanical harshness. One of the pleasures of the city is in seeing the routine skill, efficiency and speed with which its trees

off the Quai de Montebello

are pruned and looked after. I enjoy also the patterns of the cast-iron gratings which protect the base of their trunks and allow water to feed down to the roots. The shade and freshness of these trees make the wide pavements and their benches pleasant for walking and sitting. But these important amenities are threatened as the pedestrians'

160

Boulevard de Magenta

pavements are ruthlessly annexed by anything on wheels, an invasion to which everyone seems to turn a blind eye. No one much likes these parked cars and in the student riots of November 1990 I saw a lot of them burnt out.

Occasionally nature hits back. One windy night I was awakened in a hotel off the Rue des Archives by a sharp gust and the sound of splintering. Next morning I was saddened to see that one chestnut from a very beautiful clump in the street nearby had been blown over, but was glad that in the process it had squashed one of the empty cars parked on the pavement. People were inspecting it with that staggered look that acts of God provoke, but by afternoon it was already sawn up and all trace of its existence had been cleared away.

Rue des Archives

The Hôtel de Ville and the Propreté de Paris

Parisian civic pride and energy take two particularly striking visible forms. Their solid and formal manifestation can be seen in the fine Hôtel de Ville, whose spiky neo-Renaissance skyline dominates the Right Bank opposite the Ile de la Cité. It is much decorated: stone figures lie elegantly about or perch as best they can on its crowded façade, while on the crest of the roof stand six copper knights, green with age, bearing lances with stiff pennants.

Civic pride is evident too in the practical way the city is looked after. This same energetic self-respect fuels the vast fleet of green vehicles and the matching army of men which several times a day washes and cleans the streets: sprinkling, refreshing, hosing down, tidying up and sweeping away mess. The Propreté de Paris vehicles have specialised machinery for sucking up litter, blowing waste paper away and scouring out dustbins, while dedicated and eagle-eyed experts on motor bikes suck up the dogshit. This whole expensive business makes Paris look clean, well cared-for and beautiful, and makes a Londoner realise that his own city has lately become a neglected tip.

Hôtel de Ville

The Propreté de Paris

The Café de la Paix and the Place de L'Opéra

Parisian Street Life

Paris pavements are put to good use. Sometimes this seems to be more or less official, as if by right: cafés and restaurants and even shops spread far out onto their own patches of pavement. But the pavements are also used unofficially, for all the unlicensed, freelance or simply uncontrollable activities that take place there: minor commerce, buying and selling, hustling, entertaining, parking, begging and sleeping. Some of these things seem to have been going on uninterrupted forever; others, like begging, are growing more and more prevalent. Tacit time-sharing means that the streets get well used all round the clock, as the same patch of pavement is given over for example to market stalls in the morning, restaurant tables in the evening and parked cars at night. All in all it makes for lively spectacle.

Most Parisian pavements are in any case spacious and agreeable places: Haussmann meant his avenues and boulevards to be wide and in due course leafy. But, of course, the real interest of the Parisian streets is in the people – their faces and gestures, how they dress and how they behave and respond. This is what makes the familiar routine of drinking a cup of coffee or a glass of beer, at no matter what kind of café, so constantly tempting. When I began going to Paris, tables in the open air outside restaurants and cafés were unknown in London, and simply to see them out in force on the Paris pavements was surprising and delightful. Even now, whenever I go back there, the first coffee at an outdoor table has an almost ritual pleasure and significance.

Hotels too can enhance – or ruin – one's pleasure and peace of mind. I've stayed in many, some with their names so discreetly indicated that you can walk past them without noticing, others so flamboyantly lit up that to step inside is an anticlimax. The ones I like best are those that retain the air of having once been a private house.

Parisian pavements provide a platform for a variety of performers, of many skills and ages. As entertainment generally becomes more pre-packaged, impersonal, and canned, it is good to experience it live and newly-minted. But there is a darker aspect to this round-the-clock open-air spectacle, for the pavements have other denizens. In Paris, as in London, while some people have got spectacularly rich, others have got poorer, more miserable, and more hopeless – while still inconsiderately remaining in full view. Parisian tramps and beggars often look tough, hard and well able, with the help of their mean-looking and watchful dogs, to look after themselves. But many others look as though they are really having a bad time. One can harden one's heart to this but it's difficult to ignore it, impossible not to wonder what can have gone wrong.

Boulevard St Germain

Rue de Turenne

Rue des Archives

Boulevard Beaumarchais

Place du Petit Pont

Place de la Sorbonne

Place Clichy

Cafés and restaurants

For a visitor to Paris, cafés are an important aspect of daily existence, offering sunshine or shelter, refreshment or proper sustenance, as needed. They minister to one with great flexibility, coping with the day's requirements from breakfast until late at night; and also very consistently: you find more or less the same range of good light meals and drinks at all of them. I suppose a second-rate café would fairly quickly go out of business. What makes them interesting is the staff (even the gruff or reserved waiters generally thaw into amiability) and, even more, the clientele: one's fellow customers are good to watch.

To some degree they are predictable. You can be sure of seeing students in the cafés in the Place de la Sorbonne and scholars in the Rue des Archives, sure of hearing American accents as well as French spoken in the Deux Magots, and Moroccan or Algerian faces in the Rue de Flandre. The best-looking thing about a café is the waiters' standard and time-honoured white shirt and long apron, black trousers and waistcoat: it would be hard to look unimpressive in this get-up. Parisian waiters are highly professional: it seems here to be a vocation to be proud of, not a dead-end job or a lowly rung on a career ladder. The customer is allotted the basic respect to which he or she is entitled but anything more has to be earned.

Rue St Antoine

Pavement performers

In spring and summer, and wherever there are most visitors, out come the entertainers. Whether professional or do-it-yourself, they are generally of a high order, skilful, talented, well-equipped, or simply bold and determined. They are thickest on the ground on the bridges, near the Louvre, or around the Sacré-Cœur in Montmartre. Some of them have complicated and expensive equipment, like the many beautiful barrel organs; others have almost nothing. But the basic minimum always includes some receptacle – cap, box, bag, small basket – to put money in.

It's almost always music that first attracts your attention, though this may be only an accessory to a fire-eater or strong-man or to a pavements puppet show. The one I drew was an extremely simple set-up, seen first as you approached along the pavement: just a small black curtain suspended in mid-air above the puppeteer's bicycle and clearly visible legs. There was no mystery, no theatre, just someone wearing a strange glove standing by a bicycle. But from the front, when the music started to play, it suddenly became fascinating, funny and electrifying, and people sitting on the pavement or leaning on the bridge turned almost without realising it into an enthralled audience. Then the drama came to an end, the tape stopped playing, the onlookers drifted away and once more there was only a curtain and a bicycle.

Pavement puppets on the Pont St Louis

Bd. de Magenta   The Louvre   Sacré Coeur   Quai du Louvre   Ile de la Cité

Square du Vert Galant   Rue de Buci   Pompidou Centre   Quai de Conti   Pont St Louis

The Louvre   Place du Tertre   Pont au Double   Montmartre

Square St Médard   Hôtel Béthune Sully   Pont St Louis   Rue Mouffetard

Parisian pavement contrasts

Pavement performing looks as if it might be
fun. But straight begging, of which there is
plenty on the Paris pavements and in the
Métro subways, doesn't look like fun at all,
though it can – as in the Rue Berger –
appear irritatingly like pious showing-off.
Begging is so prevalent that it reminded
me of visits to Naples and Calcutta and the
Bowery, and of the streets of central
London today. It's a job that requires some
concentration but in general begging must
be a dispiriting form of work, only made
tolerable with the help of alcohol, though
enlivened by social contact and the interest
of the passing scene. Many activities do much
more harm; this one makes a curious
contrast to the lively, rather tarty streets
of the Faubourg St Denis, places animated
nevertheless by unexpected glimpses not
only of squalor but of beauty, as in the
pretty tiling of the Crystal-Hotel.

Place de l'Hôtel de Ville

Rue de Metz

Rue du Faubourg St Denis

Rue Berger

Boulevard Ornano

Rue de Rivoli

Boulevard St Denis

Boulevard de Sébastopol

CRYSTAL-HOTEL

171

Parisian hotels

The front door of the Hôtel Crillon

The Parisian hotels I tend to stay in are clean, quite comfortable, polite, friendly and correct. They have a fairly discreet front, a view out of the bedroom window if you're lucky but a blank wall if not, a lobby with potted plants by the reception desk, and a dining-room near by which only serves breakfasts, though the numerous staff have their lunch there. Luxury is confined to the glass of orange juice available on request at

breakfast as an optional extra. But the hotels I've drawn are either pretty or extremely grand. Everything about the Crillon is magnificent – vast scale, monster columns, fine stonework, cavernous doorway, manicured greenery, discreet nameplate. One might almost feel that the Place de la Concorde in front of it had been set out as the Crillon's own open-air extension. The comings and goings on

the pavement outside the Crillon are as interesting as the building itself, the whole impression one of attentive, well-co-ordinated and well-rehearsed splendour.

Not everyone in Paris can run to this sort of style. Opposite are some of the other people, equally characteristic, on the city's pavements, whose lives run on other lines.

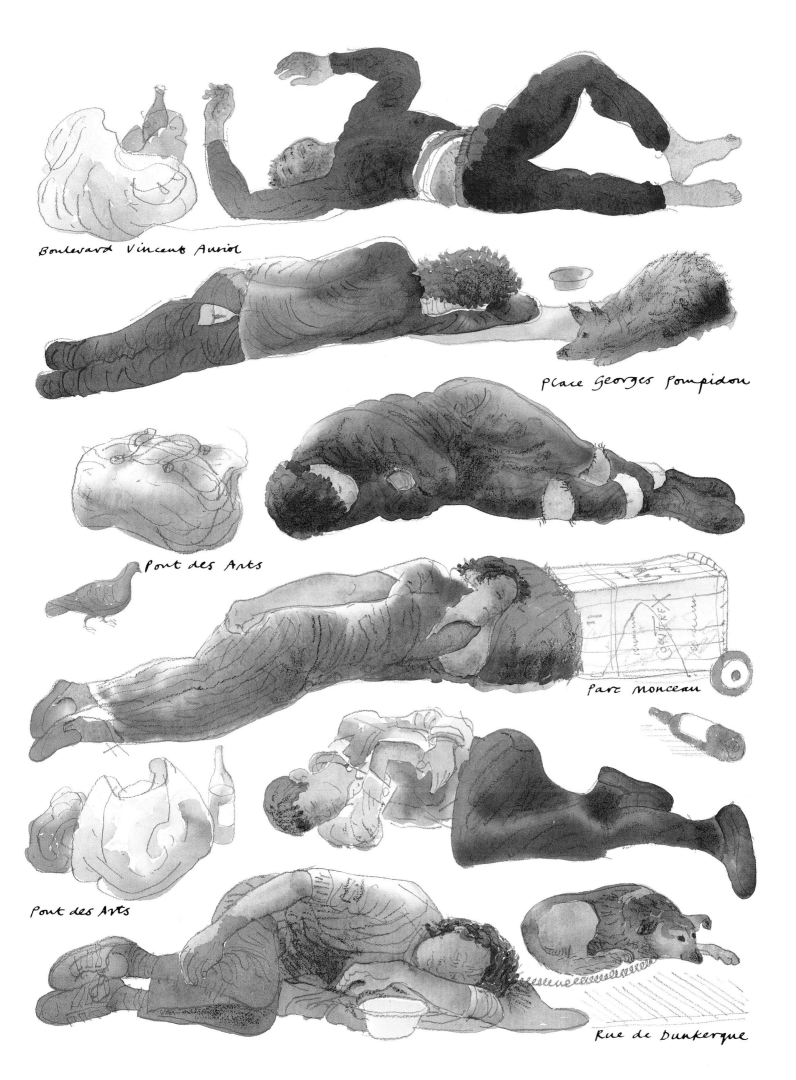

Boulevard Vincent Auriol

Place Georges Pompidou

Pont des Arts

Parc Monceau

Pont des Arts

Rue de Dunkerque

La Villette: one of the old abattoirs, now the Grande Halle

La Villette: the Géode

Renewing Paris

Left to their own devices, cities usually renew themselves willy-nilly. On the English side of the Channel it is currently unfashionable to think that anyone, or indeed anything but money, can exercise much control over the process. Paris however has gone to great lengths, not only to formulate and co-ordinate plans for its necessary development, but also to present these proposals prominently and in a way that everyone can understand. The most remarkable current manifestation of this is in the Pavillon de l'Arsenal on the Boulevard Morland, which shows by means of enormous models, diagrams, drawings and photographs how the city has developed, how its recent and new buildings are changing in tune with the spirit of the times, and how best and most intelligently it can prepare for its future. In this it contrasts dramatically with the reactionary, superficial and dilettante school of architectural criticism rife in Britain at present, criticism which reduces the subtleties of architecture and planning to a childish confrontation of goodies and baddies.

For Paris, the most intractable problems have been an efficient but elderly and saturated public transport network; the total lack of any space left to develop in the city centre; the worsening polarisation between the ever-richer western half of the city and the poor and neglected eastern half; and the need somehow to control and concert expansion beyond the Boulevard Périphérique. All this has been tackled radically and vigorously. Public transport has been improved by renewing the old Métro and plugging into it the newly-built and still-growing RER. The missing space for new development in the centre has been provided by simply digging it out – under the Louvre for the Pyramid, under the Place Igor Stravinsky next to the Pompidou for IRCAM, and under Les Halles for the Forum. The west/east imbalance has been a harder nut to crack. The drift of wealth westwards was dramatically confirmed by the creation at La Défense of a whole new commercial mega-centre. But it is being countered by the new opera house at the Bastille, by the moving of the Finance Ministry further east still to Bercy, alongside the city's new sports centre, and by the big new development – still as I write only a vast bulldozed desert of earth – beyond the Gare d'Austerlitz. The most extensive and fully realised redevelopment so far is the renewal of La Villette, the grisly old slaughterhouse region in the north-east of the city, into a park, an exhibition centre with its spherical steel Géode, and a theatre; and, related to this, the imaginative transformation of the areas surrounding the Bassin de la Villette which connects it with the centre of the city.

The remarkable thing about these plans is that in general they are not simply about pulling things down and starting again. They are more about filling in, making the best of what is already there, and also in the process accepting and even relishing some bizarre contrasts of style and some curious juxtapositions: of the old Renault factory with the vaguely futuristic Pont de Sèvres flats, of the street market under the Métro along the Boulevard Vincent Auriol with the high-rise buildings alongside, and of the tidied-up old Clignancourt flea-market with the flats beyond, flats whose neon sky signs form a new electric flea-market in their own right. But it is just such odd contrasts that make the city so surprising and, on balance, so good to look at.

Street messages and sky signs

Messages rain down on one in Paris: from the rooftops, from the pavements, from every wall, there's no way of avoiding or ignoring their information and ex-hortations. Some of them are imparted in a helpful spirit: 'This is the Place du Canada and the Pont des Invalides is that way, but we don't make a fuss about it'. Some of it is legalistic: 'This is a public place and you'd better watch your step'. Guimard's Métro entrances tell you where you are and also

convey that this is a city with some confidence, pride and a sense of style. Other signs merely serve private interests: La Samaritaine making its point reasonably enough from within its own roofline, Tati and the Crédit Lyonnais letting you know where they are in appropriate tones of voice, Daiwoo and Toshiba simply nicking any available patch of Parisian sky regardless. The French have a long tradition of open-air publicity. Big ads for Suze and St

Raphaël painted and repainted on barn walls used to add colour and vitality to the village scene, and in a notably French style: they had great character. But although I quite enjoy the visual hubbub of the Clignancourt flea market and its louche surroundings, its polluted skyline now reminds me more of a brash new city such as Hong Kong than of a distinguished and long-established European capital.

The Marché aux Puces from the périphérique

The Forum des Halles and St Eustache

Les Halles, the central markets just north of the Rue de Rivoli, used to be one of the more interesting features of central Paris. It was as if the old Covent Garden, Smithfield and Billingsgate markets had all been put side by side, under identical iron sheds, along Long Acre. And, as at Covent Garden, their removal to outer Paris left a vacuum. The Parisian solution was to dig a big hole where they'd been and fill it, partly with a new and necessary railway interchange – linking the Métro system with the fast new RER suburban lines – and partly with 'amenities' – underground shops, cafés, leisure activities and so forth. Most of these places were then covered over with grass or concrete, though some basement-level courtyards were left open to the air and light. New housing surrounds it all on the south, but to the north one's eye is held by the interesting old church of St Eustache. I find the architecture of the Forum des Halles cheap-looking and highly unsympathetic. But when the leaves are out I rather like the green-trellised pleasure garden up at street level, and at midday, on a hot weekday, the new grassy area offers real space and freshness where it didn't previously exist. There are many fountains; they smell of disinfectant.

Subterranean courtyard in the Forum des Halles
Trellised alley and St Eustache

The Bassin de la Villette

If one compares the Bassin de la Villette with
Paddington Basin one begins to understand
the vast scale of France's commitment,
historically at least, to her canals. The
Bassin is pretty empty of barges now; the
working quays and warehouses that would
have been familiar to the crew of the barge
L'Atalante have been cleared away or tidied
up and planted with trees. When I made this
drawing the two handsome warehouses at
the far end were boarded up, I assumed for
refurbishment; but the next time I was there
they were being demolished. Just beyond
them, at the Place de Bitche, is a hydraulic
bridge whose deck lifts up for boats to pass
through. Beyond it the canal continues to
the renewed La Villette itself, with its
park, its new theatre, its City of Science
and Industry, and the Grande Halle, where
cattle used to be slaughtered.

The Bassin de la Villette looking towards the Canal de l'Ourcq

The Canal St Martin and the Rotonde de la Villette

Between Métro stations Stalingrad and Jaurès, Line Two crosses the St Martin Canal and the Boulevard de la Villette. The scene offers a strange juxtaposition of buildings and of many varying kinds of transport. This drawing was made from the footbridge over the lock as a variety of craft – barges, water buses, motor boats and sailing dinghies – passed through. The lock ran with mechanical efficiency but the scene was given human interest by the glimpses of family life aboard the barges, an enviable mixture of hard work and open-air holiday.

The Rotonde de la Villette by Ledoux, on the right, is the most handsome remaining example of the ring of customs houses strung along the old Farmers-General wall. This historic wall was built in the mid-eighteenth century to mark what was then the boundary of the city, with the customs houses providing the entry points for taxable goods. The Rotonde stands now, clean and very well-restored, just where the canal widens out into the vast Bassin de la Villette, planned by Napoleon: a truly monumental undertaking. The space between the Rotonde and the Bassin used to be a lowly bus terminal but has now been splendidly laid out as a pleasure ground for the people, many of them immigrant and mostly far from rich, of the nearby working-class quarters.

183

The Canal St Martin and the Rotonde de la Villette

The Canal St Martin and the Canal de l'Ourcq

A pretty and interesting canalside walk takes in both these previous scenes, and several others just as strange. It begins just north of the Place de la République, at the Square Frédéric Lemaître (the famous actor), where the Canal St Martin emerges from a long tunnel to climb a flight of locks, each with a delicate hump-backed iron bridge, along the Quai de Jemmapes. It skirts the St Louis hospital, one of the city's oldest, whose gracious avenues and courtyards survive; they are now filled with doctors' cars and students of architecture.

The canal runs on through the Bassin de la Villette and underneath a remarkable lifting bridge. This bridge could well have turned into a disused bit of industrial archaeology. But sturdily built and mechanically sound, it is in constant use. To the east of it the waterway becomes the Canal de l'Ourcq, under which name it continues to the Parc de la Villette. Its junction with the Canal St Denis has been well laid out, with buildings and trees and water each enhancing the other. Buildings of several different periods coexist here: lowly and shabby survivors as well as tidied-up or rebuilt blocks in the local Parisian idiom, and standard international style high-rise flats. What makes this view delightful is the sense of space and fresh air, as if the canal was bringing the outer world into the great city. Quaysides, foliage and sparkling water are familiar Parisian assets. It's good that the city has chosen to make the most of them.

The Rue de Crimée bridge over the Canal de l'Ourcq

Autumn trees in the St Louis Hospital

Frédéric Lemaître and the Canal St Martin

185

The Quai de la Charente and the Canal St Denis

The changing Parisian skyline

Paris beyond the Grande Arche, La Défense

The process of renewal naturally involves striking contrasts between old and new, even when the old might itself still seem raw and intrusive. Such is the impression created just beyond the Grande Arche at La Défense, of an already ruined landscape getting a final and superfluous *coup de grâce* from yet more motorway. But such effects soften with the passage of time. The Métro along the Boulevard Vincent Auriol must itself at first have seemed a harsh intruder, but now it is treated simply as a familiar shelter for a beautiful street market – as an amenity, a bit of archaeology at the feet of the tall new flats.

Occasionally, the change is so total that there is nothing left to provide any contrast. When the old Citroën works were cleared from their riverside site near the Javel Métro, and were replaced by the flats and hotels of Front de Seine, the new took over lock stock and barrel, leaving the Citroën club barge in the river as the only visible reminder. Such curious contrasts and contradictions as there are here are internal, between the many oddly assorted and frequently ill-matched newcomers.

Saturday market under the Métro on the Boulevard Vincent Auriol

Front de Seine from the Allée des Cygnes 187

Paris from La Défense

Emerging from the RER, the spectacle of La Défense is breathtaking in its scale and rawness, its freedom from grime and from traffic. For a moment, it really does seem like the city of the future: forever new and pristine. Of course, such a city is rather limited, corporate and conformist – with all the solemn, mysterious, quasi-religious self-importance of great corporations whose essential activities, such as making cars or chemicals, go on far away in grubbier surroundings. And all the untidy clutter of domestic life, flats with washing on the line and children playing, is also absent. All in all, La Défense, with its towers and helicopters

Paris from the Grande Arche, La Défense

and basic inhumanity, reminds me of the famous set in Fritz Lang's *Metropolis*.

Its centre-piece is of course the Grande Arche: two tower-blocks of offices linked at the top by a – well, by a link. The lifts that whisk you up to the top of the Grande Arche are made of glass, and the guide-rails that steady them are light and open, so one's journey up seems almost as unprotected as if one were in a bubble. Up at the top are big enclosed exhibition areas, giving the impression of too much space and nothing to put in it. But the fresh-air view from the parapet is quite stunning – of an entirely artificial landscape of late twentieth-century tower-blocks. From this standpoint they seem to have the same simplicity, and the same solemn and careful but nevertheless arbitrary placing as children's wooden building blocks. They would be hard to distinguish without their name tags, which are more discreet than the Clignancourt sky signs but not very different. The scene is one of Haussmannesque organisation, though with this important difference: one may or may not find the spectacle to one's taste, but certainly one doesn't feel here that anything of much historic Parisian importance had to be sacrificed to make it possible. If one doesn't warm to it, it's far enough away from the centre to be ignored.

If it all looks slightly alien, it's hardly surprising. Many of the buildings belong to multinationals; the Fiat and Elf towers were designed by a Franco-American team, the Grande Arche by a Dane; even the sculptures are by the Spaniard Miró and the American Calder. There is nothing very French about this scene – why now should there be? What *is* essentially Parisian is the vigour, the conviction and the sheer nerve of the whole concept. But then, these are the very qualities that have always made looking at this astonishing city, old and new alike, such an exhilarating experience.

Place de la Concorde

Index

Italics refer to illustrations